THE NEW BOHEMIANS

THE NEW
BOHEMIANS

COOL

&

COLLECTED

HOMES

Justina Blakeney

PHOTOGRAPHY BY DABITO

ABRAMS, NEW YORK

Published in 2015 by
Stewart, Tabori & Chang
An imprint of ABRAMS

Library of Congress Control
Number: 2014942982

ISBN: 978-1-61769-151-5

Editor: Andrea Danese
Designer: Deb Wood
Production Manager: True Sims

The text of this book was composed
in Adobe Garamond, Brandon
Grotesque, and Alternate Gothic
No. 2 .

Printed and bound in the
United States

10 9 8 7 6 5 4 3 2 1

Stewart, Tabori & Chang books
are available at special discounts
when purchased in quantity for
premiums and promotions as well
as fundraising or educational use.
Special editions can also be created
to specification. For details, contact
specialsales@abramsbooks.com or
the address below.

THE ART OF BOOKS SINCE 1949
115 West 18th Street
New York, NY 10011
www.abramsbooks.com

COVER
In the guest room of Paige
Morse's home (see page 159) in
Dallas, Texas, a red suzani blanket
covers the entire back wall. Her
grandmother's slipper chair was
upholstered with a vintage wedding blanket from India. A low
mango wood table from West Elm
is inspired by a ceremonial stool
traditionally used by Bamileke
royalty in Cameroon. "The
textiles in my home cost more
than most of the furniture and all
of the appliances," says Paige. "I
tend to splurge on textiles, rugs,
blankets, and fabrics."

PAGE 1
Amhalise Morgan (see page
177) reupholstered this chrome
director's chair in woven textiles
she bought on eBay.

PAGE 2
In her art, Louise Sturges (see
page 247) experiments with
painting, photography, and
multi-media. She also prints
images on unusual media, like
this original photograph printed
onto a throw blanket.

OPPOSITE
A close-up view of the wooden
cabinet in the entryway of my
house, which I like to call the
"jungalow" (see page 275).

FOLLOWING PAGE
A plant collage on a wall in Adam
Pogue's loft (see page 263).

PAGE 8
A corner of Faith Blakeney's
living room (see page 125).

FOR IDA

CONTENTS

INTRODUCTION

WHO ARE THE NEW BOHEMIANS?

What we now understand as bohemianism emerged in early nineteenth-century France when artists moved into the lower-rent Romany (gypsy) areas of Paris as they sought out alternatives to bourgeois expectations. Artists from all over the world, most with very little income, tried to make their art and eke out a living in this part of Paris. This convergence of cultures gave rise to a kind of vagabond lifestyle, where the pursuit of wealth and other traditional indicators of success were abandoned in favor of a creative life and an active engagement in the search for alternative ideals of beauty.

This search for alternative lifestyles and aesthetics continues today—especially in response to a corporate cubicle culture that can sap the creative spirit out of anybody. Today's bohemians seek to erase the distinctions between work and play, and our living spaces reflect that lack of boundaries. The new bohemian home is a multifunctional playground for exploration and experimentation: It is an office, an art gallery, a showroom, a daycare, a photo and music studio, even a pop-up restaurant, or all of these. Our new bohemian lifestyle is rooted in freedom: free-spirited, free-form, and free of rules.

We bohemians chase free wi-fi, we blog from Brooklyn Laundromats, and we check our e-mail barefoot in Tulum. We arrive early to flea markets but late to farmers markets. We are vintage hounds. We are resourceful and profoundly creative. We are boutique owners and bloggers, mothers and makers, entrepreneurs and expats, chefs and consultants, fathers and urban farmers, doulas and dancers, collectors and curators, designers and dreamers. Our travels—whether in our own city or oceans away—inform our style. Our worldly collections are as eclectic as we are. The new bohemian is a master of layers.

LEFT The music room in Erica Tanov and Steven Emerson's house (see page 205). RIGHT The kitchen of Emily Katz and Adam Porterfield (see page 17).

MY BOHEMIAN PHILOSOPHY ON CREATIVITY

My own bohemian aesthetic arose out of my multicultural upbringing in Berkeley, California. (My father is African American and Native American of the Cherokee and Chickasaw tribes, and my mother is of Eastern European Jewish descent.) The blending of ethnic backgrounds in my childhood home gave me an appreciation for mixing things up when it came to home decor. Travel also informed my aesthetic. Every year, we got at least one new stamp in our passports, learned how to say *thank you* in at least one new language, and tried at least one kind of totally unfamiliar food (the onion ice cream in Jakarta will go down in the history books). Along with souvenirs, like a cuckoo clock from Bern, papier-mâché angels from Playa del Carmen, and a menorah from Jerusalem, I also brought back a stronger sense of self, a notion that being different was a good thing, and a pretty mean case of wanderlust that would lead me to spend ten years living abroad.

FEELING FREE

My parents weren't precious about their stuff. My siblings and I took liberties moving furniture around. I'd usurp a hutch from the hallway, lug it into my room, and convert it into a home for my winter clothes or art supplies. We were allowed to make design decisions. I remember playing hide-and-seek with my brother and sister at the carpet store when we were given permission to shop for our bedrooms. I painted murals on the walls and sewed my own curtains with some amazing mirror-ball fabric. My room was a forever-un-finished canvas, consistently evolving and being layered upon, and always an accurate reflection of me at any specific stage of life.

Under each roof that I've called home since those days in the Berkeley Hills, I've had my way with decor. In my college dorm room at UCLA, I hid with boys under layers of tented scarves and sarongs draped over and around my bed to create privacy from my roommates. When I was studying in Florence, Italy, I wanted to give my living room a Moroccan feel, so I sawed the legs down on the dining room table that came with the apartment. I'm notorious for kissing rental deposits good-bye and ushering in the freedom to make myself totally at home.

CREATIVITY IS KEY

Growing up with such freedom to design and decorate my own environment fostered my creativity and helped to shape my eclectic bohemian vibe. This sensibility, coupled with a love of sharing, compelled me to launch a design blog when I returned to the United States after seven years in Italy. And while I no longer play hide-and-seek at carpet stores (at least not lately), what has stayed with me from those formative years is that, to me, everything is creative material and nothing is too precious to make my own. Decorating is about feeling free, having fun, rejecting traditional notions about what goes with what (especially that everything in a room has to match), and getting a little bit *wild*.

I've found over the years that resourcefulness and my own imagination inspire me most. Designers discuss splurging on a $400 doorknob when for most of us, spending $400 on *anything* is a splurge. The truth is, I'm a work-ing mom, I live in a rental, and much of what I have decorated my own home with are hand-me-downs, Craigslist miracles, and thrift-shop finds. It is my strong belief that wealth is not the key to having an amazing home and an incredible lifestyle—the key is inside you; it's your own creativity and being in an environment in which you're allowed to openly express it.

In this book, my goal is to share ideas that give birth to new ideas and feed the imagination. Whether you read it cover to cover or browse for sprinkles of eye candy, my aim is to inspire you to make your home a reflection of your personality. My hope is that each time you pick up this book, it will motivate you to actually put it back down and start a new project. Switch out those tired curtains in your bedroom and layer on the fringed scarf you brought back from Spain five years ago or that sari you picked up in India. Pry open that can of paint under your bathroom sink and give that little wooden accent chair a kelly-green hue. Reupholster that cushion with a sarape. Canopy your bed in Turkish *fouta* towels, French lace nightgowns, or washed linen fabric that you dip-dyed in indigo. Let loose. Experiment. Kick off your shoes; light your incense; turn on Joni, Jimi, or Janis; and get all boho.

BREAKING DOWN THE "NEW BOHEMIAN" HOME

Though they all exemplify the new bohemian spirit, the twenty homes featured in this book are divided into six themes. The homes of the modern bohemians place a premium on clean lines and functionality. The homes of the earthy bohemians are veritable greenhouses where plants take center stage. Folksy bohemian homes are distinguished by stories of family and tradition told through art and artifacts. In nomadic bohemian homes, collections of colorful textiles reign supreme and cover every surface to evoke an almost dizzying grand bazaar effect. Romantic bohemian homes are a narrative in nature and evoke a sweet nostalgia. The maximal bohemian home (like mine!) includes a whole lot of everything.

At the end of each home, I've added a section called Adopt an Idea, which is where I offer tips and hints on how to achieve a certain aesthetic found in that home. After each of the six main sections, I've given you a couple of DIY projects that help you to bring the new bohemian vibe and spirit into your own home. In the back of the book, you'll find a plant-o-pedia that breaks down all the amazing plants and plant installations in the book and details how to care for them. The last chapter provides shopping and inspiration resources.

OPPOSITE The striking fabric wallpaper in Paige Morse's home (see page 159).

The Modern Bohemian

Whether they live in a turn-of-the-century craftsman-style house, a cabin in the hills, an urban loft, or a dome in the desert, modern bohemians mix the clean lines and functionality of classic modern design with the decorative exuberance of a bohemian. In these examples, Richard Neutra mingles with Nag Champa, Herman Miller mixes with handmade objects, and shag rugs mix with, well, even shaggier rugs.

THE **Modern** BOHEMIAN

Emily Katz
&
Adam Porterfield

PORTLAND, OREGON

Creativity oozes out of the front door of Emily and Adam's foursquare craftsman-style home built in 1906. It is their creative incubator. This two-story home, which the couple purchased in 2008, is blooming with textiles, artworks, meals, songs, furniture, and newly propagated plants. Several years and many renovations later, they are happy to be still immersed in a "never-ending process of remodeling." Emily and Adam have this to say about their house and style: "Our house is Big Lebowski meets Martha Stewart; Bob Ross meets Diane von Furstenberg; lumberjack meets *Ladies of the Canyon;* Danish modern takes a walk through the Huntington Gardens."

Emily and Adam tore out nearly every interior wall downstairs to create a wide-open space with a loftlike feel. Now there is a clear line of sight from the entryway to the kitchen, where one is likely to find Emily cooking and filling the rooms with the scents of roasted fennel, caramelizing onions, or freshly baked fruit tarts. The area is so spacious that the couple has begun to use it for events—one evening they even transformed the house into a pop-up restaurant. "We offered one fixed-price seven-course dinner with wine pairings," explains Emily.

OPPOSITE **The piano was a lucky score. "One day a friend told us about a free piano, and we had it moved here, sight unseen," says Emily. "When it arrived, we discovered that it was painted cream with little gold accents. The piano was accidentally perfect."**

EMILY KATZ
Art director, creative consultant, macramé specialist, singer, artist, and occasional fashion designer

STAR SIGN
Sagittarius, ascendant Gemini, Moon in Cancer

SPIRIT PLANT
Shiso

ADAM PORTERFIELD
Designer, screen printer, metaphysical real estate dabbler, builder and co-owner of Adventure Pipes

STAR SIGN
Aries

SPIRIT PLANT
Cannabis sativa

ON BOHEMIANISM
"Bohemian to us means focusing on working to live rather than living to work. That said, we work really hard, with adventure always on the horizon."

In the dining area, a dynamic floral arrangement designed by the couple's friend, Elizabeth Artis of Espe Floral, sits on a mirrored pedestal table. Above it hangs a classic chandelier, the only fixture left by the previous occupants.

LEFT
Perhaps it's the driftwood lamp floating overhead or the hanging chair or the massive embroidered self-portrait of Emily rising like Mother Earth from the plants and stones and crystals, but there is certainly a bit of magic in the living room, a kind of *A Midsummer Night's Dream* vibe.

BELOW
The feminine feel in the sitting area is balanced by the more masculine look of the wooden wall facing Emily's portrait. Adam reclaimed lath to adorn the wall and created a built-in area for their records and stereo. A stuffed goat head sits parallel to Emily's self-portrait, as though the two are deep in conversation. "The goat head was a gift from the amazing artist Bruce Collin Paulson of Fortress Letterpress," says Adam. "I went over to his place to pick something up and he said, 'Hey. Do you want this goat head?' Frankly, that's a question you just don't hear often enough."

OPPOSITE AND LEFT
The set of floating kitchen shelves is one of Adam's proudest DIY projects. To achieve the floating effect, Adam hid the L-bracket by burying one arm directly into the drywall and carving a slot for the other arm into the shelf itself.

BELOW
Adam completely remodeled the kitchen. He painted each wall in a different neutral hue, and a single row of Woolly Pockets is used to plant a small vertical garden above the pantry door. An Italian Fratelli Onofri gas range and oven was their biggest splurge.

Wooden shelves, countertops, and lamps give the kitchen an earthy-modern feel. "All of the wood surfaces in the house are either original, salvaged from the house, or salvaged from the region," says Adam. Driftwood pulled from the Willamette River was used to fashion the kitchen bar lamp. "We are constantly striving to bridge the gap between work and play," says Emily as she fills jars with daikon radishes for her canning club, the Portland Preservation Society, where she trades her homemade pickles with friends.

DAIKON RADISH PICKLES

I have a very early memory of my mom making these long, skinny, giant white radishes called daikon. The tangy, sour, salty flavor is my favorite.

Day One:
- Gather a large handful of daikon radishes.
- Peel the skin, then chop into rough 1-inch (2.5-cm) cubes or spears.
- Put into a nonreactive bowl—glass or ceramic is best.
- Sprinkle with about 2 tablespoons of sea salt, cover with water, place a clean tea towel over the bowl, and leave overnight on the counter.

Day Two:
1. Drain the daikon and rinse them well.
2. In a large pot, combine 1 cup (200 g) of sugar, 1 cup (240 ml) of rice vinegar, and ¾ cup (180 ml) of water and bring to a boil, stirring until the sugar is dissolved.
3. Put the daikon into two 1-quart (1-L) jars or 1 half-gallon (2-L) Mason jar.
4. Cover the daikon with the liquid, screw on the lids, allow to cool, and put the jars in the fridge.

"I eat these so fast that I never bother going through the process of canning them. Honestly I don't know how long they can keep, because I always eat them within a week! You probably will, too." —Emily

ABOVE

A collaborative textile between Emily and artist Halley Roberts is made from painted paper and embroidered tulle. Upstairs, the house has three bedrooms and two bathrooms. The first bedroom off the stairwell is used as an Airbnb room, just another way that this bohemian home can generate a little extra cash. The second bedroom is being transformed into an atelier for Emily. The third bedroom is the master, where walls were knocked out to create an open flow into the walk-in closet and master bath.

OPPOSITE

A Pendleton blanket and Turkish kilim pillows give the master bed a graphic pop while the headboard, made by a friend, includes built-in shelves.

FOLLOWING PAGE

The master bathroom is extremely open. A large interior window looks into a corner of the bedroom where Emily currently works, and a skylight and door-size window add to that open feeling. A collection of plants hangs from the rafters and injects an indoor/outdoor mood. "I love the bathtub and the window into the sitting area," says Adam. "Some of my favorite times are shared catching up while one of us soaks. That room makes my day, every day."

ADOPT AN IDEA

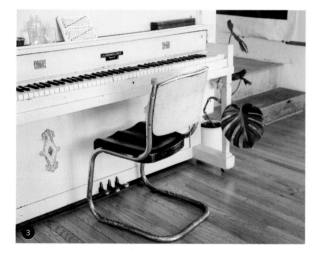

1
WOVEN WINDOW

In their guest bathroom, Emily and Adam used a Mexican weaving as a makeshift curtain. They just tied the weaving's fringe directly to the curtain rod.

2
CRATE SHELVES

In the bedroom, a wooden plank and two crates create modern storage under the windowsill, an easy, functional way to build bookshelves.

3
PAINTED PIANO

It's fun and refreshing to see a piano painted in that neutral cream color, yes? Try taking a coat of paint to your old piano—why not?

4
LATH LOVE

When remodeling, consider reusing the rubbish. Adam used lath from the walls they tore down to adorn a wall they kept up.

Josie Maran & Ali Alborzi

LOS ANGELES, CALIFORNIA

The family home of Josie Maran and Ali Alborzi is a little 1920s cabin getaway burrowed in the hills of Beachwood Canyon. Josie and her husband are the poster children for the new bohemian lifestyle—total free spirits who somehow manage to run an earth-loving cosmetics line, raise two beautiful daughters, and travel around the world. Over the years, Josie's style has migrated from bohemian-rustic to bohemian-modern, but her laissez-faire attitude and realness along with a cozy-chic flavor have remained intact. Josie often travels to Morocco, where she sources the argan oil that is the foundation of her cosmetics line. With each visit, she stuffs her suitcases with the rugs and blankets that lend Moroccan accents to her light-filled home. "We don't allow the typical cultural norms to stop us from creating our most outrageous dreams," she says.

OPPOSITE A wall of thick wooden shelves, a potbelly fireplace, and terra-cotta floor tiles make this home feel cozy.

ABOVE Josie and Ali have been living in this home since the birth of their first daughter, Rumi, in 2006. At the top of a steep flight of stairs, a wooden patio displaying a playful collection of masks and children's toys boasts a wide vista of Los Angeles.

FOLLOWING SPREAD In the living room, modern furniture blends with rustic built-ins and pops of pattern and color. Explains Ali, "We are big fans of mid-century furniture, so we rarely buy anything that is new." The rug provides a graphic edge. "We have a close relationship with the Berber tribes in Agadir and Essaouira in Morocco," says Josie. "Their women make our argan oil, and they made these rugs for us."

JOSIE MARAN
Owner of Josie Maran Cosmetics

STAR SIGN
Taurus

SPIRIT ANIMAL
Unicorn

ALI ALBORZI
CEO of Josie Maran Cosmetics

STAR SIGN
Virgo

SPIRIT ANIMAL
Elephant

RUMI JOON
Age 8

INDI JOON
Age 2

ON BOHEMIANISM
"A way of being fully alive and conscious. Of saying 'we are *free spirits!*'"

THIS PAGE AND OPPOSITE
An eat-in kitchen is warm, bright, and inviting. A fading Persian rug inherited from Ali's family softens the look of the whole room; a mid-century credenza makes up for a lack of built-in storage space; and a beautiful farmhouse sink and wood accents add to the rustic, handmade feel.

ABOVE AND OPPOSITE
Rumi's room displays a similar
mix of rustic and modern
elements. A wall of wooden
built-ins is juxtaposed with a
bright kantha quilt, colorful
animal garlands, and a modern
chair.

FOLLOWING PAGE
In the bathroom, a black-and-
white claw-foot tub sits next
to a rustic custom-built sink.
A Turkish *fouta* towel completes
the look.

ADOPT AN IDEA

1
THE REFRIGERATOR COVERED

Ali made this wooden refrigerator door by cutting and staining slats of repurposed wood and then drilling them right into the door. He then added the hardware and transformed the refrigerator in just one weekend.

2
TOY STORY

Matching bins in the shelves in the living room provide storage for the kids' toys. Having a set place for toys in the living room means that they aren't scattered all over the house.

3
HANG WITH ART

Try hanging pictures inside the shelves.

4
RUGS IN THE WASHROOM

Use a small rug in the bathroom instead of a bath mat.

Marika Wagle

NEW YORK, NEW YORK

Marika Wagle brings the colorful chaos of a souk to the clean lines and open spaces of a Tribeca loft. The decor is a delightful mix of modern and pop with textiles collected from her world travels, rugs she inherited from her Indian father, and modern pieces that give it that New York City edge. "In my home, I love the feeling of 'just a little too much.' People say when you are leaving the house, you should look in the mirror and remove one accessory. I say add one! Sometimes that can feel overwhelming to people, but it keeps me stimulated and inspired."

OPPOSITE
Fish-eye views of the loft reflect off of two Tom Dixon pendant lamps suspended over the dining table. The sleek, modern design of the pendants echoes through-out the space with its graphic prints and mid-century Lucite coffee table Marika inherited from her grandmother. But these clean, modern lines are just the framework for a contrasting explosion of personality, pattern, and color.

ABOVE
The window facing the sofa is covered in Berber pillows picked up in Morocco. "In Marrakesh, I visited the Jardin Majorelle, the gardens made famous by Yves Saint Laurent," says Marika. "I was inspired by the brilliant shade of blue named after Majorelle and used throughout the gardens. When I found some metal lanterns in the souks later that day, I had them painted to match that perfect color."

MARIKA WAGLE
Fashion merchant

STAR SIGN
Leo

SPIRIT ANIMAL
Monkey. "I'm a little mischievous and wild, but at the end of the day I just want to cuddle."

ON BOHEMIANISM
"Bohemian to me means unconventional and free-spirited. A risk-taker. I don't think it's a particular aesthetic, but more an attitude of doing what's true to you without apologies and without fear."

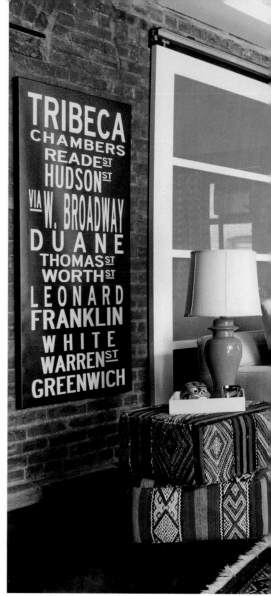

ABOVE
Artwork and family photographs adorn the walls in the dining area, and the sleek furniture is covered with colorful tablecloths, suzani blankets, and woven baskets. "I have a general fear of solids," says Marika. "I love bringing pattern into my home and the easiest way to do that is with tapestries or throws. I have everything from Mexican wool blankets to Indian embroideries and Moroccan kilim pillows—I love blending all those cultures together."

OPPOSITE ABOVE AND BELOW
The riot of pattern and color continues into the living room. The sofa is covered with a contemporary throw from Calypso St. Barth and a collection of modern, graphic pillows. Stacked Moroccan poufs covered in woven Berber fabrics, used here as a side table, hold a bright yellow tray and orange table lamp. Indian rugs passed down from Marika's father are spread out on the floor, where some floor pillows and a suzani-covered ottoman invite guests to lounge about the homey space. "I try not to take it all too seriously," says Marika. "I love to have an element of humor and play—like my papier-mâché cow's head. It is perfectly ironic because I am vegan." A transparent Lucite coffee table holds a very modern—almost pop—vignette: art books, a papier-mâché skull, a little bronze stupa, a cowrie-shell beaded box, and a neon-toned handwoven vintage Berber basket.

ABOVE AND OPPOSITE
Behind frosted glass doors, Marika's bed is a celebration of suzani. "The headboard is made from a vintage piece I found in a little shop in Udaipur," says Marika. "I had my upholsterer make it into a headboard, and the extra fabric was used to make steps for my Chihuahua to get onto the bed."

RIGHT
Hidden behind the headboard is a built-in vanity. Marika's personal style is reflected in her wild collection of beads and baubles.

OPPOSITE
A gallery of artwork by her niece makes the industrial-style kitchen one of Marika's favorite spots in the house. "When she was three years old, she came to stay at my apartment for about a month," says Marika. "She's a brilliant artist—according to her totally objective aunt!—so every time she made something, I stuck it up on my cabinets with this great neon paper tape. By the time she left, all the cabinets were covered. That was about two years ago, and I'll probably never take them down."

ABOVE
In the bathroom, Cavern Home Navajo wallpaper packs a graphic punch.

FOLLOWING PAGE
Marika's small office holds a sofa covered by a sarape. Two large art pieces fill the walls: an abstract paper-cutout piece by Zac Buehner and an art piece that Marika put together herself. "It's an old contact sheet from a modeling shoot of my grandmother in the 1960s," explains Marika. "I had a printer blow it up and stretch it onto canvas."

ADOPT AN IDEA

1	2	3	4
LET'S BE CLEAR	**PARASOL PERFECT**	**CREATE A WALL**	**POP ART**
Pick clear elements—like Marika's vintage Lucite coffee table—that allow patterns on the rugs to show through.	Use a parasol to cover a wall sconce.	If you're short on wall space, float your bed in the center of the room and use the headboard as an additional wall. Then use space behind the bed to maximize storage.	Take a series of favorite photos or a contact sheet to a print shop and have it copied onto large-format paper. Black-and-white large-format prints are surprisingly affordable. Mount the image itself on the wall or frame it.

Katherin & Brian Smirke

JOSHUA TREE,
CALIFORNIA

When Katherin Smirke put an ad on Craigslist looking for a cabin in Joshua Tree, a man immediately responded about a 1980s-era geodesic dome going on the market the very next day. It seemed written in the stars. Katherin and her husband drove out to the desert to check it out, and they went into escrow that week. After nine months of renovations—scraping out popcorn ceilings, stained rugs, and rat poop—the dome was ready for smoldering sage and good company.

KATHERIN SMIRKE
Owner of Gypsan

STAR SIGN
Aquarius

SPIRIT ANIMAL
Owl

BRIAN SMIRKE
Real estate redeveloper

STAR SIGN
Pisces

SPIRIT PLANT
Joshua tree

ON BOHEMIANISM
"A willingness to embrace our free spirit and live life on our own terms. It also represents a joy in creating and enjoying life, and a positive and nurturing spirit."

OPPOSITE
Light spills into the cool space from the glass of the door, illuminating a simple butterfly chair and an oak stump side table they rescued "from a firewood vendor's chainsaw." Most of the decor comes from Katherin's obsession with Craigslist. "As soon as our offer was accepted, I implemented a plan to buy as many unique and interesting items I could possibly find," she says. "I stalked Craigslist night and day, quickly filling the garage in our LA home as well as our spare bedrooms. I think Brian was starting to lose it a little because we were living like hoarders toward the end of our project."

ABOVE
Approaching the dome feels magical. The quiet of the desert is almost absolute, and the large Joshua tree next to the home seems to curtsy and smile. The bright yellow frame on the front door beckons.

ABOVE
Inside, the eye is drawn up to the
five skylights, Katherin and Brian's
most costly alteration.

BELOW
Polyhedral planters resting on the
stump echo the shape of the dome.

A potbelly fireplace spray-painted silver sits on the sidelines. A mid-century couch faces the "television," which in this house means a large window open to the desert panorama. Glass terrariums on a vintage slat coffee table are very desert-modern. A chair Katherin salvaged from the street and reupholstered makes the space cozy. Pops of yellow are omnipresent in the dome.

OPPOSITE
A white kitchen from Ikea is given a cosmic-boho vibe with colorful accents. Rainbow knives and a bright yellow toaster keep the space playful and personal.

BELOW LEFT
A simple piece of cotton is cut into a circle and used as a table-cloth on a tulip-base table from CB2.

BELOW
A turquoise space-age bird feeder nourishes little birds that can't believe their luck.

OPPOSITE
Off the bedroom, an addition provides a space for writing, hanging out, or resting.

ABOVE
Above the daybed hangs a graphic print and faux stained glass decals on the window. "I love when the sun hits the decals and reflects the shapes onto the walls, which creates a piece of art in itself," says Katherin. A sarape from Brian's childhood, dream catchers, and small thrifted rugs complete the room.

FOLLOWING PAGE
In the bedroom, the dome's unusual shape presented both challenges and opportunities. On the one hand, it was difficult to find art that fit comfortably on the angular walls. But ultimately, this challenge was an engine for geometric inspiration. They also made the triangular hanging shelf, and the polyhedral art on the wall behind the bed. The cross-stitch fabric at the foot of the bed is actually a poncho from Katherin's vintage clothing collection.

ADOPT AN IDEA

1
BRIGHT
ACCENTS

Pick one bright color to weave throughout the space. Pops of yellow bring a happy, colorful highlight to this space without being overwhelming.

2
CHECK
CRAIGSLIST

Anything can be found on Craigslist, from Ikea furniture to high-quality vintage pieces to domes in the desert. The online flea market should always be a first stop for shopping.

3
DIY
DECALS

Katherin made the faux stained glass from sheets of vinyl stickers. She cut the stickers into triangles then stuck them to the windows. This is especially great if you're short on wall space.

4
UPSIDE DOWN
YOU TURN ME

An affordable basket from Target becomes an even more affordable side table. Turn a rigid basket upside down to get the look.

SHIBORI-DYED BOXES

TIME: Weekend

ESTIMATED COST: $45

DIFFICULTY: ✳ ✳ ✳

WITH NATALIE GLUCK MITCHELL

I grew up in Berkeley, California, where our city flag may as well have been tie-dyed. Both the process of tie-dyeing and the outcome are fun and unpredictable, and I love the look of the watery patterns spread over textiles. I'd tie-dye my whole world if I could! This versatile storage box is inspired by the bedding in the Dome and the Japanese tie-dye technique called shibori. It was designed with the idea that the boxes could hold and hide anything from files to shoes to extra blankets or towels and help keep a space free of clutter while still looking pretty and put together.

NOTE: Make sure to wear rubber gloves and to work in a well-ventilated area when handling the dye.

MATERIALS

Indigo dye. The Indigo Tie Dye Kit from Jacquard is a favorite.

100% cotton canvas fabric

2 adjustable C-clamps—from your local hardware store

Cardboard storage box with lift-off lid

Mod Podge

SUPPLIES

Rubber gloves

5-gallon (19-L) plastic container

2 pieces craft plywood sheets

Heavy-duty wide rubber bands

Foam sponge brush

Scissors

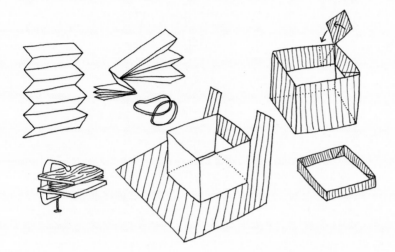

INSTRUCTIONS

1. Using rubber gloves and the plastic container, follow the dye preparation directions for the indigo dye kit you chose.

2. While the dye is setting up, prepare the fabric using one of the following techniques. We used two different binding techniques, but the possibilities for resists are endless.

   Accordion-fold technique: With the accordion-fold technique, the result is a loose striped pattern. Fold the fabric back and forth in narrow strips so as to create an accordion. Then fold the strip of fabric in half. Sandwich the folded fabric between two pieces of plywood and use the clamps to secure the layers together. Tighten the clamps as much as possible.

   Banded-accordion technique: With the banded-accordion technique, the result is a pattern of "bleeding" squares. Using the technique

above, accordion-fold the fabric back and forth in wide strips, then accordion-fold it again so that the final shape is a square, not a narrow rectangle. Tightly wrap several wide rubber bands around the fabric bundle. Be sure they cross each other in many different places to create a random spiderweb pattern.

3. Soak the bound fabric in water, then revisit the directions specific to your dye. Follow those instructions. Once your fabric is completely dry, move on to step 4.

4. Wrap the cardboard box bottom as if wrapping a gift, applying Mod Podge with the foam sponge brush to adhere the fabric to the box as you go. Cut slits at the top corners of the fabric, fold the flaps of remaining fabric inside the box, and glue with Mod Podge. Follow these same steps with the box lid.

5. Once dry, fill with unsightly items and none will be the wiser!

SHIBORI

In Japan, the earliest evidence of shibori techniques dates back to the eighth century. Hemp, silk, and later cotton was folded, twisted, creased, stitched, and braided and then dyed in blues from the indigo plant, reds from the madder plant, or purples from the purple beetroot resulting in ethereal, cloudlike patterns. The word "shibori" comes from the Japanese verb root "shiboru," meaning "to wring, squeeze, press."

DRIFTWOOD WALL SCONCE

TIME: Less than 30 minutes
ESTIMATED COST: $30
DIFFICULTY: *

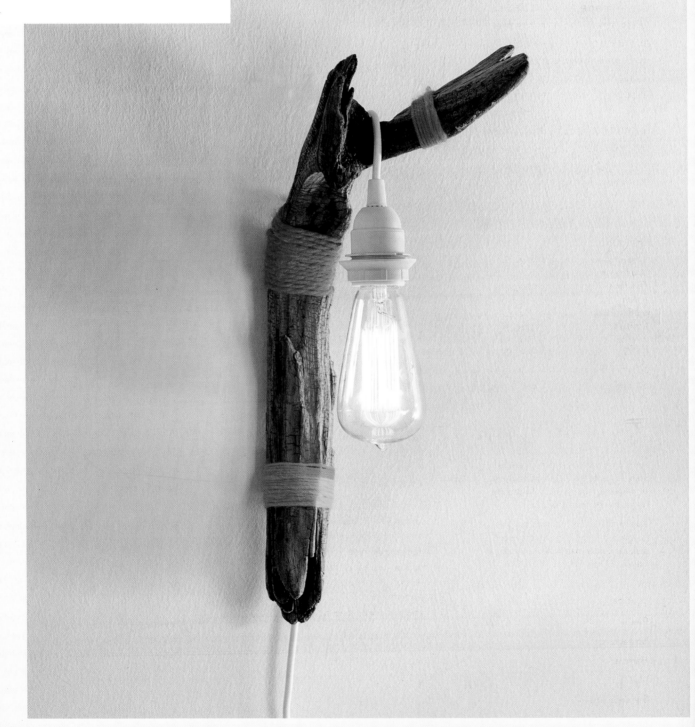

I love all of the drift-wood lamps in Emily and Adam's craftsman-style home. When I spoke with them about how they were made, it sounded so easy that I had to create a version for myself. I love the simplicity of this driftwood wall sconce, but I couldn't resist adding my own flavor to it—I injected a bit of color with yarn. It would be fun to paint it, too, so go for it and get all boho on the driftwood.

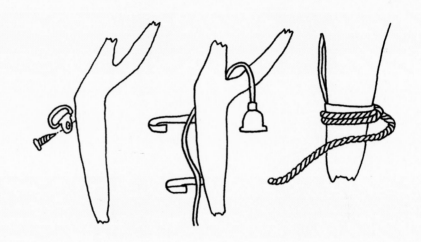

MATERIALS

One long, lean piece of driftwood. You may need to look around a bit to find the perfect shape. I'd love to say I found this in a local river, but the truth is I bought it on eBay for $12. Driftwood is sold for use in aquariums, so in addition to your local river, you can forage in your local pet shop for the perfect piece.

One light socket and cord set. I used the Hemma cord set in white from Ikea.

Ring hanger with screws.

Filament light bulb. This project wouldn't work without a filament light bulb. It's pricey, but the antique look of it elevates the project and actually makes it look more modern.

Yarn in a few colors. I used orange and yellow, because that's my vibe, but pick the colors that work with your space.

SUPPLIES

Pencil

Screwdriver

Hammer

Nail

Electrical tape

INSTRUCTIONS

1. Experiment a bit with the wood and light socket. Figure out how you want the piece of wood positioned on the wall. With the wood set as you like, mark the tallest point that makes contact with the wall on the back and at the same time mark the wall. Screw the ring hanger into the back of the wood at this spot. Hammer a nail into the spot on the wall.

2. Place the light bulb in the socket. Place the cord on the desired point of the driftwood so that the light is suspended at a height you like.

3. Remove the light bulb and attach the cord to the back of the drift-wood by wrapping the electrical tape around both the cord and the body of the driftwood in a few locations. (The tape will eventually be covered by yarn, so place the tape where the yarn will go.)

4. Tie a long strand of yarn around your driftwood just below the first piece of tape (make sure the knot remains to the back) and carefully wrap the driftwood in yarn, making sure to cover the tape. Take creative freedom with the amount of yarn you wrap and the colors you use. Tie the yarn in a double knot at the back when done. Repeat on other areas of the wood, as desired.

5. Replace the light bulb and hang the sconce on the wall.

The Earthy Bohemian

Nature rules. The earthy bohemian home is full of foresty fancies: rattan and wool, plants and pets, earth tones and weathered woods. Relaxed and airy, informal with rustic details, the earthy bohemian home is just the place for those whose feet are on the ground but whose heads are in the stars.

THE Earthy BOHEMIAN

Anne Parker
&
Alea Joy

PORTLAND, OREGON

What do you get if a handy prop stylist shares an apartment with a plant-loving floral designer? You get a home that's full of fancy flora, perfect pottery, and pops of pattern. It's an inviting mix—the kind you get only by selecting your roommate based on aesthetic compatibility, as was the case with Anne and Alea. They bring different things to the table stylistically, and while their bedrooms exemplify their individual styles, the rest of the home is a perfect blend of Anne's handmade-rustic sensibility and Alea's romantic whimsy. Together, they've created a home that is earthy, cozy, and lovingly cultivated. Alea says, "I seem not to be able to resist anything plant, stone, bone, or feather." About her own style, Anne says, "I collect baskets, pottery, wooden spoons, kilim pillows, sheepskins, wool blankets, plants . . . Basically, whenever I decide I like something, I can't stop buying different versions of the same thing."

OPPOSITE
The dining room is the heart of this home. The table and bench were handmade by Anne at her father's nearby workshop and provide a perfectly *informal* formal dining setup. A vibrant wall of plants exudes good vibes. A large hutch that came with the home anchors the space and makes the room feel somewhat grand. Anne's jars of pickles and preserves together with Alea's wild floral arrangements enliven the room's earthy palette, while the rug provides a pop of pattern.

ANNE PARKER
Prop and food stylist

STAR SIGN
Aries

SPIRIT ANIMAL
Cat, "probably because there is nothing I like more than to be cozy."

ALEA JOY
Floral designer and co-owner of Solabee, a plant/floral boutique

STAR SIGN
Gemini

SPIRIT ANIMALS
Vulture/Fox

ON BOHEMIANISM
According to Anne, "A bohemian is someone who defies convention and doesn't fit in a box. I don't see it solely as an aesthetic classification, but more of an approach to life."

Anne and Alea rent the entire bottom floor of a triplex built in 1910. "It's been pretty well preserved in its original state," says Anne. "It retains some charming details, like glass doorknobs, leaded glass windows, picture rails, built-ins, wood floors, and high ceilings. In the summer, I basically live on the front porch, which is a great perk of the house."

OPPOSITE AND ABOVE

The living room presents a mix of natural textures and colors: a jute rug, a rattan side table, burl and driftwood accents, leather, sheepskin, linen, and a whole lot of happy plants. "Alea and I both grew up in rural Oregon with hippie parents, and I think that has helped inform both of our aesthetics," says Anne. "I am drawn to natural materials and fibers, and neutral colors. Alea, on the other hand, has a bit more of an eclectic taste and likes color more than I do, but there is a lot of overlap between us. Plants are at the crux of that common interest." The vintage couch, chair, and coffee table by Brazilian designer Percival Lafer were all lucky Craigslist finds.

**PREVIOUS PAGE,
BELOW, AND OPPOSITE**
The bones of the narrow kitchen are like any standard rental apartment, but the copper pots, uniform jars, and wooden accessories lend charm to the small space. More charming still is the adjacent breakfast room with its tall, open wooden shelving filled with handmade bowls, pottery, breadboards, cake stands, teapots, and collections of wooden spoons from Anne's international travels. A mid-century brass lamp, and a chest of drawers reside, somewhat unusually, in the eating area—but the result is both visually compelling and inviting.

THIS PAGE AND OPPOSITE
Off the breakfast room is Alea's bedroom, where rainbows, crystals, dream catchers, bird's nests, and an archer's bow make the room feel adventurous and romantic. The back wall is the palest of pinks, and hanging nightgowns evoke a certain delicate femininity. A plant collection at the window adds a bit of drama. "I tend to arrange around my plants, making sure they have good light," says Alea.

FOLLOWING PAGE
Anne's bedroom is like a tiny jewel box. One dark wall creates mood while the remaining white walls and white ceiling ensure the room doesn't feel too cavelike. What stands out here is texture—a headboard covered in jute, a fluffy sheepskin, plants, and twigs and branches. Anne's vibe is as much about how things feel as how they look. The natural elements are juxtaposed with pops of metallic— a brass lamp and a poster in black and gold.

ADOPT AN IDEA

1
SKINNY SHELVES
ABOVE THE BED

Both Anne and Alea have
skinny floating shelves above
their beds. A nice solution
for storage and display, the
shelves are a great way to
draw the eye up and make
the room feel larger.

2
WINDOW
WIN

It can be tough to know how
to decorate around a low
window, so when in doubt,
add plants! Plant an indoor
garden on a low bench: The
plants will get the light they
need, but you'll still benefit
from the light, too.

3
BUILT
TO FIT

When it comes to shelves,
custom builds may be the best
option. This shelf looks so
good because it fits the space
perfectly. It also fits their
stuff nicely—Anne raised the
bottom shelf just enough to
accommodate her rain boots.

Mileece Petre

LOS ANGELES, CALIFORNIA

Turning a parking lot into an oasis sounds like a mammoth project, one that would need tractors and contractors, landscape architects and engineers. So how did a waiflike English "sonic artist" transform this mid-city concrete yard and garage into a plant sanctuary? With the help of Craigslist, sweat equity, and an endless capacity to follow a dream. "My home is found, nurtured, bled over, sweat over, cared for, endlessly reworked, and endlessly generous."

MILEECE PETRE
Sonic artist, environment designer, and renewable energy creator

STAR SIGN
Gemini

SPIRIT ANIMALS
Dragonfly/Beaver

ON BOHEMIANISM
"Opium dens and the idea of being equal parts intellectual and sensitive."

OPPOSITE
Mileece had the idea to convert the garage and lot behind her mother's 1930s Spanish home into an indoor/outdoor haven after using the space as a makeshift music studio. The sun beat down on the concrete lot, and Mileece wanted trees that would provide shade and breathe life into the space. Her mother thought she was crazy, but she ultimately welcomed the additions. Seven years and a whole lot of work later, the addition of a "few trees" turned into an indoor/outdoor urban oasis of lush vegetation, including fruit trees, an edible vertical garden, and a pond full of fish and turtles.

FOLLOWING SPREAD
For most of the year, the garage door remains up to reveal a sheltered lounge area that is open to the patio. "I love the plants smothering my eyes with bursts of green!" exclaims Mileece.

ABOVE AND RIGHT
An eclectic array of chairs and sofas
surrounds a wooden table home-
built by Mileece and her husband,
Nathaniel. Plants grow freely into
the home, blurring the distinction
between outside and in.

Mileece created this bookshelf in the garage lounge by cutting directly into the drywall and adding some horizontal beams and painting the drywall in various shades of fiery red.

OPPOSITE AND LEFT
The bathroom feels like a rainforest. Air plants and bromeliads, which love the moisture and humidity that showers bring, seem to grow right out of a wall covered in tree bark.

BELOW
Bamboo wallpaper brings the green into another room that triples as a music studio, guest room, and closet.

ABOVE AND OPPOSITE
In her studio, Mileece makes music with plants. She developed software that translates the plant's electromagnetic currents into musical notes. She accomplished this by attaching electrodes directly onto the leaves. Imagine an orchestra of bromeliads and philodendrons—the music produced is ethereal, mysterious, and beautiful.

"What do I love about my home? The birds, the birds, the birds singing to remind me of the glory of Earth! The leaves in the dancing light! The flowers, the flowers, the indescribably alluring flowers, and the magical scent that hangs in the air. The cat, the silly little turtle, the constantly pregnant fish, the snails, the strange and beautiful bugs, my bed, my piano, and my kettle."

THIS PAGE, OPPOSITE, AND FOLLOWING PAGE The space is also home to an Airstream that Mileece bought from an elderly couple for $2,000. It was a total wreck when first purchased and took nearly a year to restore and renovate. Now it functions as a bedroom and quiet workspace. Occasionally, Mileece lists the Airstream on Airbnb for extra income, or simply lends it to traveling friends.

ADOPT AN IDEA

1	2	3	4
DIG IN	A TALE OF TILLANDSIA	PUT THIS IN YOUR PIPE AND PLANT IT	GARAGE MIRAGE
Save space by building bookshelves directlyinto your walls.	Use air plants in your bathroom to get a tropical vibe.	Use pipes to create a vertical garden for edibles.	Remember, even a space as unremarkable as a garage can be transformed into a magnificent sanctuary!

Emily Baker
&
Kerby Ferris

PORTLAND, OREGON

In the Portland bungalow of Emily Baker and Kerby Ferris, a bright white backdrop is offset by layered patterns and natural collections of foraged finds. For this creative couple, there is little distinction between nature and art. "We both do yoga and meditate and rest here. It's not a party or gathering space. It's our sanctuary, more for focusing and regrouping. We write music here together, make art, and share space in solitude here as well."

OPPOSITE
Portland can be gray much of the year, so Emily and Kerby chose a sunny-yellow paint to brighten up what could have been a drab kitchen. By painting only half the room, the space is bright but remains sophisticated. A versatile rustic table is used for extra counter space but can be extended into a breakfast table when necessary. The ikat rug recalls the blue door and dominates the old linoleum. Sticks of lemongrass provide a pop of green and are used for tea. Many people would have discarded a slice of old rug and a bit of buoy, but here, two castaways become captains of the kitchen, adding a splash of visual interest to the walls.

FOLLOWING SPREAD
The interior of this small, stand-alone home in Portland's Alberta Arts District is fragrant with eucalyptus and sage, an earthy smell reminiscent of the forests that hug the Oregon coast. The decor evokes a place where forest meets beach—bright and airy, thick with plants and moss and driftwood, organic shapes, and a feeling of openness. "We wanted to create a home that felt like Luke Skywalker's aunt and uncle's house on Tatooine," explains Emily. "A celestial greenhouse, a romantic holodeck, a rainbow meditation space with plants filling our minds with clear energy and warmth and green raindrop happiness. We wanted to keep the living room open, so we have sparse furnishings," says Kerby.

EMILY BAKER
Jewelry designer,
owner of Sword and Fern boutique

STAR SIGN
Taurus

SPIRIT ANIMALS
Bear/Dolphin/Spider

SPIRIT PLANTS
Hamamelis virginiana
(witch hazel), sword fern,
and *Magnolia grandiflora*

KERBY FERRIS
Musician, sound designer

STAR SIGN
Cancer

SPIRIT ANIMALS
Fox/Cat/Mouse

SPIRIT PLANT
Euphorbia

ON BOHEMIANISM
"We think of ourselves as free-spirited life hackers, crystal peacemakers, mindful disco lovers, with future rainbow prism hearts."

BELOW
True to new bohemian form, the home of Emily and Kerby includes a workshop dedicated to their various crafts: jewelry making, homeopathic medicine, and music. Emily makes jewelry to sell at her tiny boutique, Sword and Fern, which also features other cosmic, one-of-a-kind oddities, as well as her wild-crafted medicinals.

OPPOSITE
Emily pushes her jewelry-making practice in a novel direction by making oversize pieces for display as a fun departure from prints or textile art. Fashioned from wood, beads, and rope, these enormous statement necklaces are the perfect adornment for the walls of her home.

RIGHT
Layered rugs, a couple of crates, and two birch tree stumps create the perfect transformable setup.

ABOVE LEFT
Emily also makes herbal incense. "I source herbs and plants locally and dry them, then prepare blends. I blend resins and leaves to create scents for different rooms and moods. My favorites are eucalyptus, Douglas fir, and black copal."

ABOVE RIGHT
Shelves throughout the home display collections of natural objects, such as stones, stumps, clay pots, and plants. They all function as sculpture. Large rocks are thoughtfully arranged with a Druid's eye, piled on top of each other, and smaller stones live in bowls, like candy. Plants, wildflowers, and shells—all are arranged with purpose. Each rock, shell, and leaf evokes memories for Emily and Kerby. "Our natural collections are from our travels to Joshua Tree, Columbia Gorge, and the Oregon coast," says Emily. "I feel bad about it, but I take rocks from the coast. The crystals mostly come from estate sales, where I buy the collections of elderly rock hounds. There's a lot of quartz, pyrite, and agate in Oregon." Plants are perched all over the home, but for Emily and Kerby, it's not only about the aesthetics. "Plants are important to us because of the health and stress-management benefits," explains Emily. "I have a deep connection to the plant world, and I use only plant-based medicines, naturopathic remedies, and herbs to cure and prevent any illnesses for me or my family, even my pet. I am a wild-edible-medicinal-plant nut!"

CREATE YOUR OWN HOME FRAGRANCE

The fragrance of lavender is believed to encourage gentle love. Mugwort is burned to enhance dreams. Sage is known for its cleansing powers, and rosemary induces happy memories and is said to improve concentration. To create a home fragrance like Emily and Kerby do, follow these simple steps.

1. Gather some herb stalks: bay leaves, lavender, mugwort, or sage (or create a combination).

2. Clip the stalks of fresh leaves to 6 to 10 inches (15 to 25 cm) long.

3. Bundle the stalks and tightly press them together. Use a natural-fiber twine or string (try cotton) to tie the bundle around its base. Leave a 3-inch (7-cm) tail coming off of the knot.

4. Wrap the bundle with the string while pressing the stalks together. Wrap continuously all the way up the bundle, and when you reach the top, go all the way back down. Tie the string around the end of the bundle once or twice, then cut it off, leaving a 3-inch (7-cm) tail. Tie the two tails together to finish the wrap.

5. Hang the bundles upside down in your home to dry for about 2 weeks. Once dry, fill a bowl halfway with sand, place the herb bundle in the sand, and burn in a safe place.

6. Enjoy the good vibes.

LEFT

A piece of furniture crafted from items that Emily and Kerby picked up at a local salvage yard houses their natural collections. It was their first "3-D collaboration." Another of Emily's wall necklaces hangs above the shelf.

BELOW

Instead of a traditional window treatment, Emily and Kerby draped a heavy, printed piece of linen casually over the window.

OPPOSITE

It took a lot of work to create this open and inviting atmosphere from the original space they first rented. "When we moved in, every room was covered with paint of the same color: a ridiculously mind-numbing industrial prison shade of Malibu Barbie Band-Aid," says Emily. "It was scary and depressing."

FOLLOWING PAGE

Emily and Kerby slumber in good humor. The boob pillowcases are made by Gravel and Gold, and the bedcover was bought at Ikea.

ADOPT AN IDEA

1
BASKET CASE

A basket by the couch can hide additional blankets or remote controls.

2
WHAT A CRATE IDEA

Besides being an affordable alternative to a coffee table, crates provide additional storage. Also, they can be moved around into endless configurations. Paint the crates white to give them a beachy feel.

3
ONE FOR ALL, ALL FOR ONE

Large rugs can come with a heavy price tag, so layering smaller rugs can be an affordable and visually stimulating way to cover more ground.

4
PUT NATURE TO WORK

Natural objects as functional decor—crystals as lamps, stumps as tables, plants as window treatments, foraged wood as a floating shelf or a place to hang jewelry. The possibilities are limited only by your imagination.

HANGING PLANTER

TIME: Less than one hour
ESTIMATED COST: $5
DIFFICULTY: ✱ ✱

I believe that plants increase the quality of life at home, breathe life into boring corners, and even help with air quality, so I like to fill my home with them. This means I have plants on the floors, tables, and, yes, hanging from the ceiling! In this simple, no-sew project, a piece of vinyl is easily transformed into an earthy bohemian plant hanger with a sweet tassel and a fun pop of yellow!

MATERIALS

One 30" × 30" (76 cm × 76 cm) piece of yellow or other color vinyl. I got mine at a local fabric store in the remnants section. You can also use leather.

S hook or screw hook and wall anchors, for hanging

SUPPLIES

Photocopier

Scissors

Masking tape

Cutting mat

Craft knife

Hot glue gun

BODY PIECE A

TASSEL PIECES

B

A

C

HANGING STRIPS

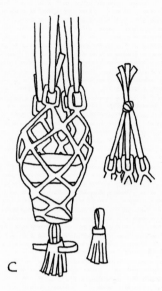

INSTRUCTIONS

1. Enlarge the Body Piece A template (see page 302) by 4 times on the photocopier and make 4 copies.

2. Cut out each copy and tape the pieces together to create a full circle template for the body of the hanger.

3. Lay a piece of vinyl slightly larger than the template on the mat. Attach the template to the vinyl with masking tape. Using the knife, cut through both the template and fabric along the internal black lines, working inward. Then cut around the edge of the template. Don't forget to cut out the marked holes in the 4 flaps.

4. Cut 2 parallel slits each ½" (12 mm) long in the center of Body Piece A.

5. Cut a 8" × 3" (20 cm × 8 cm) piece from the vinyl (see Tassel Diagram). Cut the fringe as shown in the diagram.

6. Cut a 5" × ½" (12 cm × 12 mm) piece from the vinyl. This will be the strip to hang the tassel from the planter (Tassel Piece B). Glue it to the top edge of Tassel Piece A so that 4" (10 cm) stick out from the top.

7. Place a strip of hot glue along the top of Tassel Piece A and roll it up so that Tassel Piece B is enclosed.

8. Thread Tassel Piece B up through one of the slits made in step 4 and then down through the other so that the tassel is hanging from the bottom of the plant hanger.

9. Cut a 3" × ¾" (7.5 cm × 2 cm) piece from the vinyl (Tassel Piece C).

10. Hold Tassel Piece B against the body of the tassel and glue Tassel Piece C around it, securing the tassel to the bottom of the plant hanger.

11. Cut four 30" × ½" (76 cm × 12 mm) strips from the vinyl (hanging strips).

12. Thread the hanging strips through the holes made in step 3 and glue each one in place by folding it back onto itself and applying hot glue to the end. Be sure the correct side of the vinyl is showing on the outside.

13. Tie the hanging strips together at their tops in a simple knot.

14. Use an S-hook to hang the planter off of a curtain rod, or add a screw hook into the desired location with wall anchors, and carefully place a plant in your new spiffy hanging planter.

TRIPOD PLANTER

TIME: Less than one hour
ESTIMATED COST: $40
DIFFICULTY: *

Tripod planters are statement pieces that add a cool retro vibe to a room or patio. Succulents have shallow roots and store water in their leaves, so you can create a succulent planter from almost anything. This planter is inspired by the modern lines in Anne and Alea's home, as well as the indoor gardens and use of wood in all three earthy bohemian homes featured here.

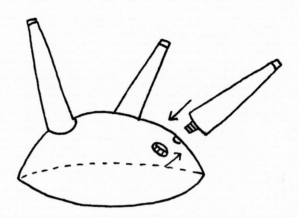

MATERIALS

A wooden bowl. I used Ikea's Rundlig serving bowl. I love the green color it comes in, and the bowl is the perfect size, shape, and price ($13)!

Three wooden peg legs with screws attached. These are easily purchased on eBay or Etsy for around $20 for a set of four; use search terms like "tapered furniture legs" or "furniture peg legs."

Three nuts that fit over the screws on the peg legs

Potting soil for succulents

A collection of succulents

Craspedia flowers (billy balls), dried or fresh (if you use fresh flowers, they will dry in the pot)

SUPPLIES

Tape measure

Pencil

Drill with drill bit

Wood glue

INSTRUCTIONS

1. Turn the bowl upside down on a clean, smooth surface. Measure out and mark where you want the legs to go. The distance will vary depending on the size of the bowl and legs. Remember that you want the legs to angle outward a bit, so mark the holes far out enough on the bowl that the legs will protrude at an angle, but not so far that the planter starts to look like a spaceship! Make sure that the holes are equidistant from each other and from the center of the bowl.

2. Drill a small hole at each mark. The size of the hole should be just shy of the size of the screws that are attached to the tapered legs.

3. Drill a couple of additional small holes in the bottom of the bowl for water drainage to prevent root rot.

4. Cover the flat surface at the top of each leg with wood glue, then screw the legs into the holes designated for the legs. Secure the legs by screwing the nuts onto the screws inside of the bowl.

5. Fill the bowl almost to the brim with the soil. Plant the succulents and water them. (Don't water them again until the soil is completely dry.) Add *Craspedia* flowers (billy balls) for a little pop of yellow, and admire your sweet mid-century-style planter.

The Folksy Bohemian

When a home is so full of arts and crafts that it blurs the line between *maison* and museum, you've entered the home of the folksy bohemian. Their homes revolve around family. Heirlooms and keepsakes take center stage. Every piece of art comes with a story of a grandmother or a quirky family trip. Packed with tales of adventures, treasure hunting, and hand-me-downs, the folksy bohemian is a collector, a maker, an upcycler, and a storyteller.

THE Folksy
BOHEMIAN

Stella & Pedro Alberti

LOS ANGELES, CALIFORNIA

There is something magical about the home of Argentine artists Stella and Pedro Alberti. One can sense it even before entering the home, as Pedro has created a colorful little mosaic on a patch of grass at the sidewalk. It is a Gaudí-esque moment that whispers to passersby, "Here's a little something I made by hand to make you smile." The absence of window treatments invites one to peek inside this 1920s Spanish-style home, and like the little dioramas that Stella meticulously creates, every little detail of the home is just so. The scent of freshly baked bread says, "*¡Bienvenidos!*" Stella remarks, "What do I love about my home? The sunshine. We face south, so the sun is always shining in our house."

OPPOSITE The front patio—a bricolage of Pedro's and Stella's handiwork and sensibilities—provides the perfect palate cleanser in preparation for the charm that awaits inside.

ABOVE A chestful of wooden pieces may seem like a work in progress or like some collection of junk picked up at a salvage yard, but in fact, they are sculptural heirlooms. The wooden legs at one time held up Stella's grandparents' bed; the violin back comes from her uncle's studio in Córdoba, Argentina. "I love collecting pieces of wood," says Stella. "Old pieces of furniture, wood carvings—anything made of wood."

STELLA ALBERTI
Designer, artist, couturier

STAR SIGN
Aquarius

SPIRIT PLANT
Lavender

PEDRO ALBERTI
Artist

STAR SIGN
Sagittarius

SPIRIT ANIMAL
Human

ON BOHEMIANISM
"It's freedom . . . a bohemian person is someone who feels a little bit free, like I do."

ABOVE
The heart of this home is the dining room, where seven wooden chairs surround a large wooden table. The chairs are all different in design, but the wood in all pulls them together. On the wall behind the table hang some of Pedro's collages from the 1970s. They are hung in a grid, which creates a collage effect.

OPPOSITE
Just inside the front door, one gets a sense of the carefully curated atmosphere of the entire house. A low table holds neatly organized bits and pieces, such as antique irons and keys, weathered bottles, and yerba maté gourds, all gathered from the couple's travels, culture, and history.

OPPOSITE

Stella loves to entertain, as evidenced by how many cooking and eating areas there are: a breakfast room and a formal dining area inside, as well as a kitchen and dining room outdoors—all in a small two-bedroom home! French bistro chairs and a row of small plants perched on wood blocks give this bright breakfast room a European bed-and-breakfast feel.

ABOVE

In the kitchen, Pedro installed bright blue tiles as a backdrop for the handmade wooden cabinets and floating shelves. Petite mugs Stella began collecting in Mexico in the 1970s hang from hooks screwed into a strip of wood. The open shelving puts Stella's collections of dishes and cups on display. A greenhouse window welcomes life and light into the kitchen. Stella keeps bouquets of freshly cut herbs here, so scents of rosemary and mint mingle with the aroma of fresh bread.

In the living room, a vintage Mexican blanket covers the back of a simple Hovas sofa from Ikea. Dress forms are ready to model new pieces from Stella's bridal collections. Though packed with art and furniture, the white walls, tall windows, and grand archways keep the room feeling open but with plenty of old-world charm.

RIGHT AND BELOW
Stella converted a second bedroom into a studio. An old credenza holds rows of little glass jars full of sewing notions, boxes of silk flowers, a collection of buttons like you've never seen, lace, pom-poms, tulle, linens, and gauze. A half-finished wedding dress hangs on the door. A veil in progress lounges on the sewing island. Piles of textiles from travels to Turkey, Morocco, Mexico, and Peru are hidden away in the cabinets. Using only one sewing machine, Stella crafts one-of-a-kind pieces fit for bohemian brides everywhere. (I came here for many a fitting when she made my own boho wedding gown a few years ago!)

OPPOSITE
Pedro converted the garage into an art studio, where his enormous double-sided paintings are rigged to the ceiling on rails so that they can be pulled out and assessed from all angles. High shelves and rows of drawers hold pigments and paints, brushes and photographs, all at the ready for the artist's use.

OPPOSITE
Wood is used as an accent color here—the bedside tables, the curtain rods, and doorframes keep the bright white room looking homey. A muslin gown, one of Stella's works in progress, hangs in the doorway with a dream catcher and a collection of vintage lingerie. A little desk is used as a vanity and the mirror above it is surrounded by photos of her children and grandchildren.

ABOVE
A simple bedroom is given personal touches with the use of textiles. An embroidered silk Spanish fringed scarf is used as a bedspread, and a kilim rug Stella picked up in Istanbul adds a pop of color to the room.

FOLLOWING PAGE
Instead of using this skinny walkway for garbage bins and outside storage, Stella and Pedro have transformed it into a magical mosaic patio garden with its own kitchen, complete with sink, barbecue, and pizza oven.

ADOPT AN IDEA

1	2	3	4
MINI MUSEUM	SAVINGS, SQUARED	HOOK UP YOUR MOSAIC	WINDOWS, DOORS, MIRRORS

1 MINI MUSEUM

When organizing your collections at home, cluster similar items together. Try organizing them by height with taller items behind shorter items. Be sure to leave space between items to let them "breathe."

2 SAVINGS, SQUARED

Pedro tiled one corner of the bathroom with cement tiles, framing the claw-foot tub. Cement tiles can be quite pricey, but with this arrangement, you get the effect of the patterned tile without covering (and paying for) the entire bathroom floor.

3 HOOK UP YOUR MOSAIC

Loops and handles from broken mugs in Pedro's mosaics make great hooks for cooking utensils or rags.

4 WINDOWS, DOORS, MIRRORS

On the patio, Stella and Pedro use old, salvaged windows, doors, and mirrors to create the illusion that the patio is larger than it is.

Faith Blakeney

LOS ANGELES, CALIFORNIA

Faith Blakeney, my big sister, taught me most of what I know about being a bohemian. I watched her layer brass bangles, burn sage, and bargain at flea markets long before I bangled, burned, or bargained. The home that she shares with her daughter, Noa, is a perfect reflection of her sense of humor, art, and the importance of family. "The vibe in our home is intended to nourish a sense of intimacy, comfort, and belonging," says Faith. "I was inspired by the playful, cozy intimacy of a tree house or Bedouin tent. My dream is to have several charming, funky homes, in my favorite cities all over the world—and maybe to swap them with friends so we can all feel at home all over the place. Who's in?"

OPPOSITE Faith and Noa's home, lovingly referred to as the Treehouse, is a turn-of-the-century "in-law"—a small apartment on the second floor of a house that is accessible by an outdoor stairway leading up to a separate entrance, which was intended for visits from the in-laws. In this case, a steep flight of stairs leads to a small patio, where outdoor rugs, chairs, and potted succulents look out over the neighborhood. When the glass doors in the living room are open, the salty breeze blows in from the nearby Pacific Ocean. Inside, faint stripes are painted onto a slanted ceiling, evoking a circus tent.

FAITH BLAKENEY
Interior designer, fashion stylist

STAR SIGN
Leo

SPIRIT PLANT
Moroccan mint

SPIRIT ANIMAL
Cougar

NOA
Age 7

ON BOHEMIANISM
"Living on the forefront. Being tapped into what is happening culturally, and dancing on the edge of it, to your own rhythm. It's a lifestyle of free thinking, free spirit, art, creativity, and passion."

BELOW AND OPPOSITE
The Treehouse displays some quirky architectural details, like sloped ceilings, which create little nooks and niches. Furniture, found mostly at thrift shops and flea markets, remains fairly low to the ground, and the violet kilim rug, sheepskins, and floor pillows invite guests to kick off their shoes and chill out on the floor.

BELOW
The mid-century arc lamp belonged to our great-grandfather. Faith found the butterflies at a flea market and mounted and framed them herself.

FOLLOWING SPREAD
At one end of the living room is Faith's bed nook, painted in a warm mauve reminiscent of the desert. The space is separated from the living room by a double curtain rod that holds kantha quilts and voile fabric. Tassel trim from Turkey is draped across the doorway, adding another layer of interest and privacy.

OPPOSITE
The pom-pom lamp was found at the Long Beach flea market. At the time, Faith found two of these lamps—the other one is in my living room! The art above the sofa tends to change from week to week, as Faith buys and sells pieces regularly for clients.

ABOVE
Floating shelves hold cherished collections. "I am a treasure hunter," says Faith, "and my daughter is a primo artiste. So our home is sprinkled with art and knickknacks from our adventures. We collect crystals, kantha quilts, cool picture books, art of all sorts, and hugs."

ABOVE
The watercolor-streaked plates
were found at the Long Beach flea
market. The quirky portrait of
our father in the background was
made by our uncle, but it was our
mother who added the real hair to
the portrait.

OPPOSITE
Another little nook functions as
a dining room. Painted in warm
gray, the dining area feels open
despite its small size. The shaggy
rug, pedestal table, and mid-
century bucket chairs work
together to create a modern look,
while the framed art by friends
and family keeps the space folksy.

OPPOSITE AND ABOVE
Faith says, "I have a gypsy soul, so
I make sure that travel is a big part
of mine and my daughter's life.
She has traveled to more than ten
countries and I, to plenty more. I
adore Rome, Havana, Brooklyn,
Paris, and Berkeley. If I have it
my way, our next adventures will
include Argentina, Israel, and
South Africa." Artworks, including pieces by Noa, and family
photos are displayed throughout
the small kitchen, and a fringed
scarf acts as a window treatment.

FOLLOWING PAGE
In Noa's room, a large fringed
scarf is tacked to the ceiling
to create a canopy. A vintage
dresser is painted canary yellow,
and the ceiling is painted a cool
periwinkle.

ADOPT AN IDEA

1	2	3
WOODEN COATRACK	SCARVES AS CURTAINS	QUILTS AS CURTAINS

An old piece of wood and a collection of hooks create a simple coatrack for the entryway.

In the kitchen and in Noa's bedroom, lacy scarves are hung as window treatments, adding whimsy. They also cast pretty lacy shadows when the sun shines through them.

Turn any fabric into a curtain with simple curtain clips. Kantha quilts are especially nice because they generally have varying patterns on either side.

Mattie Kannard & Dennis Smith

LAS CRUCES, NEW MEXICO

Las Cruces is a small town in New Mexico just upriver from the border towns of El Paso, Texas, and Ciudad Juárez, Mexico. A sense of cultural crossroads is palpable in the region and particularly notable in the folksy bohemian home of the Kannard-Smiths. The boxy little house where Dennis, Mattie, and Mackie live was built in 1912 by Dennis's great-uncle, and has remained in his family ever since. They use their home as a workshop, and each year, they harvest pecans from their orchard. Says Mattie: "I am drawn to border towns. They have that unique mix of cultures that underscores how impermanent borders really are. People, culture, music, aesthetics, and art just flow back and forth in spite of the walls people build. Border towns demonstrate the power of people's tastes, values, and inner lives, running like water through the cracks and crevices of man-made boundaries."

"When I was a little girl, I'd often dream of a cozy house full of animals, color, and life. My life in this little *casita* is beyond anything I ever dreamed of. This house is our family's nest," says Mattie. A clutter of cats, wily little dogs, happy hens, and rogue roosters are all part of the Kannard-Smith household. Laundry sways as it dries on a line in the New Mexican breeze. A collection of tiles waits to be transformed into a mosaic. The yard is at once a farm, a workshop, and a place of leisure.

MATTIE KANNARD
Middle school teacher

STAR SIGN
Scorpio

SPIRIT PLANT
Mother-in-law's tongue,
"because they're hard to kill."

DENNIS SMITH
GIS specialist, or mapmaker

STAR SIGN
Aquarius

SPIRIT ANIMAL
Ocelot, their tomcat

MACKIE
Age 13

ON BOHEMIANISM
From Mattie: "I've always been comfortable letting my soul, my heart, and my creativity guide me. Life is art, an aesthetic experience, a connectedness. Our home is a reflection of that."

PREVIOUS SPREAD, LEFT
The ornate front door of the Kannard house opens into a living room that feels like a folk-art gallery.

RIGHT
The greenhouse was their biggest splurge. "Every year, so many of my plants would die over the winter," says Mattie. "Our house is too small for them, and we don't get good light. So I ordered a greenhouse kit and Dennis made a short foundation wall so that it ended up with a higher ceiling. I love it, and it helps me winter my beloved plants!"

ABOVE AND OPPOSITE
Inside the house, the eye feasts on rich color. Collections of art and artifacts, textiles and dolls, religious iconography and masks, as well as random, bright, delightful odds and ends, are all on display like a jolly chorus. A rattan basket hides extra bedding and functions as a coffee table.

"Visitors often compare our house to a museum," says Mattie. "I am not very good at editing, so our look is a bit of a hodgepodge." Still, Mattie never loses sight of the meaning of the place itself. "I want Mackie to continue to have roots in this house and this land," she says. "Our house is like a member of our family now; it has grown with us, changed as we've changed, and has inspired us to create, design, and live with the things we love."

LEFT AND BELOW

The dining room is between the kitchen and the living room, and one must pass through it to get to the bedroom area, so it really feels like a crossroads—a border room, if you will—that bridges all the rooms in the house, both physically and stylistically. Ceramic is a dominant theme here. The family took day trips into Juárez to handpick each tile used to create both the mosaic atop the dining table and the backsplash behind Grandma's potbelly stove. Inside the display cabinet are collections of Mexican *talavera* pottery.

OPPOSITE

A thrifted armchair in the corner of the dining room is reupholstered with a Mexican Saltillo sarape and paired with a kilim-covered footstool. Blue ikat-printed curtains from West Elm recall the blue in the accent pillow and the stool used here as a side table.

PREVIOUS SPREAD AND THIS PAGE

In the kitchen, cookware and cutlery are on display with dolls, masks, and paintings. A rooster-shaped planter sits at the kitchen window where her real roosters often hop up for a peek inside the kitchen. The white wall and vintage white stove, which Mattie found for $10 at a local thrift shop, ground the space and keep it feeling bright and airy.

FOLLOWING PAGE
Mattie and Dennis wear tattooed wedding rings, and signs above their bed read, "I love that you are my wife" and "I love that you are my husband." Airy curtains fashioned from drop cloth keep the room romantic. The enormous wood cabinet built by Dennis holds more of Mattie's collections.

ABOVE
Perhaps it has to do with her affinity for borders, but Mattie loves to decorate her doors: Her bedroom door is completely covered in *milagros*; her front door is painted yellow with a blue frame and a floral motif; and her bathroom door is covered in a blue and yellow petal pattern.

RIGHT
Mosaics in the showers, hanging plants, and a collection of thrifted painted landscapes add charm to the bathroom.

ADOPT AN IDEA

1	2	3	4
PAINTED FRAMES	**DROP IT LIKE IT'S HOT**	**PEGBOARD IN THE KITCHEN**	**BRING THE INDOORS OUT**

Mattie painted a red frame around each of her living room windows. This helps make the windows appear larger and provides a graphic punch behind the striped curtains.

Affordable drop cloths are used in the bedroom as curtains. They do a great job of diffusing the light and could pass for expensive linen.

Mattie used white-painted pegboard to hang and display her tools and art in the kitchen. For those of us who are lacking in kitchen storage, this is a fun and functional solution.

Mattie and Dennis use indoor furniture, like weathered cabinets, on their patio. It helps to give the patio a decorated feel and also helps with storage.

MOSAIC RACK

TIME: Weekend, plus additional drying time
ESTIMATED COST: $20
DIFFICULTY: ✱ ✱ ✱

In both Mattie's and Stella's homes, mosaics are more than simply aesthetic: The grout holds memories of the families coming together to make something special for the home—a backsplash for a fireplace, a wall of a pizza oven, or a detail in the sidewalk in front of the house. This little mosaic is also more than just aesthetic; it functions as a little rack for a kitchen or bathroom, and it is also sentimental—I broke one of my favorite tea cups, so I decided to use it as the jumping-off place in this piece. Now my favorite broken tea cup can be a soap dish or a little succulent planter.

MATERIALS

A good mix of old ceramics, including plates and cups. Plates are good because flat pieces work best. Cups or mugs are good for their handles—try to find mugs with handles of different shapes and sizes for visual interest and functionality. Small handles can be placed horizontally on the board to become holders for utensils; large handles can be used to hold dishcloths or washcloths. For this project, I used five old mugs and two saucers. I chose to go with a blue-and-white color scheme, and I picked ceramics with varying patterns. I find that mixing solid and patterned pieces within a limited color range makes for the most successful piece, but have fun choosing the color and pattern scheme that works best for you.

A wooden board. Can be any size, but make sure the board is at least ½" (12 mm) thick. The ceramics and grout get heavy, so the board needs to be strong enough to hold the weight. For my board, I used a plain small wooden shelf, which worked really well because it has a nice beveled edge that makes the finished product look polished.

Ring hangers with screws

Tile adhesive. Make sure that the type of adhesive you get will adhere tile to wood.

Grout

SUPPLIES

Towel

Paper bags

Protective goggles

Hammer

Sandpaper

Paper bigger than the dimensions of the wooden board—try cutting open a paper bag

Pencil

Screwdriver

Spreader knife

Painter's tape

Rag

Nails

1. Place one ceramic mug wrapped in a towel inside a paper bag. Don your safety goggles, place the bag on a cement floor, and hammer the mug just once or twice, taking care not to hammer where the handle of the mug is, because you want to keep the handle intact.

2. Open the bag and towel and look for the piece with the handle and set it aside. Also take out any pieces that are a good half cup so that you can create a holder like I have on my rack. After you've taken out the good large pieces, continue to hammer the mug into smaller fragments—try to keep the sizes ranging from the size of a dime to the size of a silver dollar (½" to 2"/12 mm to 5 cm across). Don't go crazy—you don't want the mug in a million fragments.

3. Repeat steps 1 and 2 with the rest of the ceramic pieces until you have all of your hooks and at least one holder, plus plenty of filler pieces. You'll want some open hooks and some closed hooks, so it's OK if some of the hooks break while you're hammering.

4. Sand down any super-sharp edges on the handle and holder pieces. They should be smooth to the touch before you move on to the next step.

5. On a piece of paper, trace the shape of the wooden board. Carefully create your arrangement on the paper. When arranging the pieces, it's helpful to put down the handle pieces first, then fill in the rest like you're doing a jigsaw puzzle. As you create your arrangement, think about the functionality of your piece—where you want to put it and what you want it to hold. Is it for keys and a coat in your entryway, or toothbrushes and soap in your bathroom?

Answering these questions first will help to define the placement of the hooks. Closed handles placed horizontally on the board can serve as holders for utensils like spoons and toothbrushes, and if you place them vertically, you can use them to hold dishtowels, hand towels, or scarves. Also, using the original edges of plates or mugs at the edges of the wood will make nice smooth edges for the rack.

6. Examine your layout. If there seems to be too much ceramic around any of the handle pieces, or if any of them feel just too big or too curved, place the piece inside the towel and gently tap the excess off with the hammer (be sure to protect your eyes with protective goggles).

7. Screw the two ring hangers onto the top back corners of your wooden board.

8. Spread a layer of adhesive on the front of the board.

9. Move your design, piece by piece, from the paper onto the board.

10. Let the pieces dry thoroughly according to the package directions. (The adhesive I use has a 48-hour drying time.)

11. Put tape around the perimeter of the board and spread the grout onto the board like you're frosting a cake. Fill in all the cracks between the pieces with the grout.

12. Once all the cracks are filled, use the rag to remove any excess grout and wipe all of the pieces clean. Watch out for sharp ceramic edges that may be sticking out. You will find that different pieces are different depths, so you may have to dig a little deeper in certain areas to clean off the more shallow pieces.

13. Let the grout dry fully according to the package directions. This can take a couple of days.

14. After the grout is dry, remove the tape and sand down any protruding and/or sharp edges.

15. Mark the placement on the wall and hammer nails for each ring hanger. Hang your new mosaic rack!

TASSEL TRIM DUVET

TIME: 2 hours
ESTIMATED COST: $100
DIFFICULTY: ✳ ✳

There's something about tassels, fringe, and pom-pom trim that can turn something a bit "ho-hum" into something kinda "boho-yum." In this project, a boring yet affordable duvet cover gets a makeover with a little folksy bohemian flair. Tactile and whimsical with a hint of opulence, this simple project can easily be applied to any duvet already in your home.

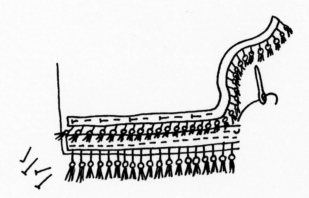

MATERIALS

Duvet cover—this is the king-size Dvala duvet cover from Ikea ($35)

Tassel trim. I got this trim at Michael Levine Fabrics in downtown LA, but it can also easily be found online at places like Tassel Outlet on Etsy (tasseloutlet.etsy.com) and generally costs around $10 per yard (meter). It's best to measure the actual duvet, but here is an approximation of how much tassel trim you'll need for various sizes:

Twin: 120" (305 cm)
Full: 160" (406 cm)
Queen: 180" (457 cm)
King or Cal King: 210" (533 cm)

Thread to match the tassels

SUPPLIES

Sewing pins

Needle and thread (or sewing machine)

Scissors

INSTRUCTIONS

1. Machine-wash and dry the duvet cover according to the label. Machine-wash the tassels in a laundry bag on cold. Tumble dry on the no-heat cycle.

2. Pin a row of tassel trim to the bottom edge of the duvet cover.

3. Using a straight stitch, sew the top edge of the tassel trim to the duvet cover by hand or with a sewing machine, removing the pins as you go. Then sew the bottom edge of the tassel trim to the duvet cover.

4. Pin a second row of tassel trim 1" (2.5 cm) above the first row. Sew the top and bottom edges of the tassel trim onto the duvet cover, removing the pins as you go.

5. Cut off any excess tassel trim on either side of the duvet cover.

In the Middle East, tassels were worn as talismans, especially on hats and hoods, to protect people from evil spirits.

The Nomadic Bohemian

When the spirit of the vagabond takes hold of the aesthete, the result is a nomadic bohemian, whose vibrant home is packed with textiles, ephemera, and anything else picked up during travels in both the actual and virtual worlds. Their homes are about movement: Objects, furniture, and even entire rooms are constantly being relocated. Things move in, out, and about the homes as much as their inhabitants do. Travel is vital.

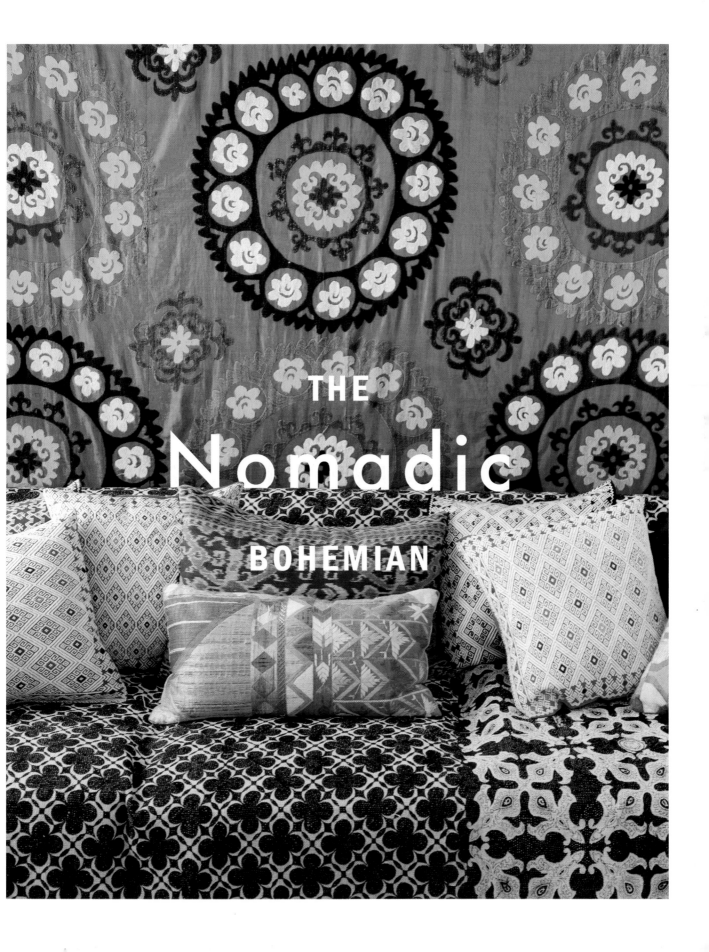

THE
Nomadic
BOHEMIAN

Paige Morse

DALLAS, TEXAS

Paige Morse's quaint turn-of-the-century home sits on a tree-lined street in Dallas, Texas. Her home is as sophisticated as it is comfortable. Each room is painted in moody shades of gray so that her beloved patterns and worldly objects pop off the walls. "I am a prop stylist for my profession, so I have lots of stuff," says Paige. "I have it displayed on rotation in my home. I also have a garage and two sheds full of all the things I just can't live without. More substance than fuss, but beauty is paramount."

PAIGE MORSE
Photo and prop stylist, interior designer

STAR SIGN
Gemini

SPIRIT PLANT
French lavender. "It is hardy, beautiful, and wonderfully fragrant, and it thrives in tough conditions."

ON BOHEMIANISM
"Choosing to live a life less ordinary. It means you aren't influenced by social norms and pursue a life that fulfills your senses. You follow your whims. Even when you're poor, life feels rich. You travel without an agenda. You immerse yourself in other cultures. You surround yourself with things that remind you of where you have been and what you have experienced. You love nature and the earth with awe and respect and seek to be surrounded by it and bring it into your home. Patina and decay are as beautiful as objects that are fresh and vibrant. You follow rhythms, not schedules, You appreciate everything that is rich with spirit, soul, and story."

OPPOSITE
In Paige's bedroom, an old table acts as both desk and bedside table. A mix of thrifted and discount-store treasures pop against the dark wall.

ABOVE AND OPPOSITE
"I spend a lot of time planning out where the furniture should be placed so it is inviting and comfortable and every seat has a good view," says Paige. In the living room, a broad coffee table displays little collections of studied objects, including a graphic beaded Yoruba crown. "I travel often and am inspired by the culture and aesthetic of the places I visit and want to incorporate that into my living space," says Paige. A vintage painting of a pink sunset discovered at a garage sale hangs above an inherited couch reupholstered in blue velvet and accented with kuba, kilim, and kantha pillows.

ABOVE
The dining room is eclectic and borrows pieces from many eras and pockets of the world. Paige's grandmother's 1960s round maple dining table has been painted black. The wishbone chairs add a bit of classic modern feel to the space and are left in their original finish to provide contrast with the table. A peacock chair adds a bit of 1970s funk. The kilim rug was purchased at Wisteria while she was working with the creative team there. The table lamps, though purchased at Lamps Plus, also have a 1970s feel. The vintage *toran* window valance brings a bit of India into the room. When asked whether her home fits her personality, Paige replies: "My house and style might look a little older and more serious than I actually am. The only thing that may not come across is that I am drawn to antiques and vintage pieces even though I'm fairly young. I usually have hip-hop music blasting and late-night dance parties down in the kitchen."

OPPOSITE
A colorful Moroccan rag rug was found at Nannie Inez design shop in Austin, Texas, where Paige grew up. Another *toran* window valance points to a windowsill full of happy succulents. "I love fresh citrus smells," says Paige. "I save all my orange, lemon, and lime peels and leave them in the kitchen sink to make the whole kitchen smell of citrus."

BELOW
In the bedroom, a Bamileke feather headdress hangs above a button-tufted headboard. Also known as a juju hat, it is traditionally worn by chiefs and dignitaries on important occasions in Cameroon. Paige chose black for the walls partially to fulfill a teenage dream of having a black bedroom, one that her mother would never abide. "I didn't want to just move in and decorate everything in a flash," says Paige. "I wanted to be deliberate and purposeful about each piece I chose, where I would put it, and how I would use it. I didn't choose which bedroom would be mine until I had slept in all of them for extended periods to determine how the light would be in the morning, the heat would feel in the summer, or proximity to the kitchen and bathroom would feel. I ended up choosing this room without a closet because I like the morning light here the best."

FOLLOWING PAGE
In the hallway, Paige often rotates the items that cluster around the wooden Ganesha.

ABOVE
Paige's favorite red suzani turned pink during a laundry misadventure. It was a happy accident, however, as the resulting pink is unusual and striking against her peach velvet armchair.

OPPOSITE
Paige painted a two-dollar junk-store chandelier black and white to match the color scheme in the bathroom.

ADOPT AN IDEA

1	2	3	4
GOT IT COVERED	**BRING IN THE BURLAP**	**PLANT MARKER**	**LOVELY LAUNDRY**

I love how Paige uses this fabric as wallpaper and even hangs artwork over the top of it. It creates depth and layers and so much visual interest.

While normally used for holding rice, here burlap makes a comeback as curtains. It's an affordable and very easy solution that protects privacy but also welcomes the sun.

Paige scored this sweet planter at a discount store, but its pattern gave me a DIY idea: Why not take a black permanent marker to a white planter?

Commercial packaging can often make a room look junky. Paige uses a large jar and vintage mug to store and scoop her laundry detergent. It's old school and chic!

Michela Goldschmied

LOS ANGELES, CALIFORNIA

It's hard to imagine a home more bold and confident than that of Michela Goldschmied and her family. Their Hollywood Hills home is a decor experience full of art, pattern, texture, and a healthy dose of color. The high ceilings allow for bolder choices than most homes, but Michela manages to bring it all together in a strikingly harmonious way.

MICHELA GOLDSCHMIED
Fashion designer, interior designer

STAR SIGN
Aquarius

SPIRIT PLANT
Orchid

ON BOHEMIANISM
"Bohemian means to follow your own mind and spirit."

OPPOSITE AND FOLLOWING SPREAD
Every single wall of Michela's living room is a different bright color: turquoise, magenta, lavender, and the tallest wall is covered in bold red brocade wallpaper. But the color crash doesn't stop there: A green ikat-printed sofa, two velvet settees (one red and one purple), a suzani-covered ottoman and some saturated Turkish rugs are added to the mix, resulting in a room exploding with color. One of Michela's talents is how effortlessly she mixes one-of-a-kind and designer pieces with affordable items from big-box stores. Her velvet settees are from Urban Outfitters while the pillows resting on them were custom-made from a kilim rug bought at a bazaar in Istanbul. "In this home, it's not so much about individual pieces, as how they all work together. Despite the myriad colors, for example, red accents are woven throughout, as seen in the rugs, pillows, lamp shades, doors, and the brocade wallpaper. The matching curtains and the repetition of Warhol collages all add to the overall cohesiveness.

ABOVE
In the bathroom and bedroom upstairs the playful mix of teal and lavender brings a vitality and freshness to the rooms. The Moroccan bathroom tiles are reminiscent of a hammam.

OPPOSITE
The periwinkle breakfast nook provides a light-filled intimate space for the traditional Italian *colazione*.

FOLLOWING PAGE
In the foyer that leads upstairs to the bedrooms, vintage swag lamps create an intimate feeling. A painted, thrifted credenza with new hardware sits underneath paintings from Michela's childhood home.

ADOPT AN IDEA

1
DRESS UP
YOUR PATIO

Use a bold-colored sheer fabric to create mood and shade in an outdoor area.

2
A TWEET
IDEA

Rig a light inside a birdcage to create a romantic, sculptural pendant lamp.

3
A GOOD
WRAP

Wrap an ottoman in a suzani blanket and top it with a Moroccan silver tray to create a coffee table.

Amhalise Morgan

BROOKLYN, NEW YORK

Amhalise Morgan lives with her two kids, Harmony Cree and Rebel Spirit, in a turn-of-the-century brownstone in Bedford-Stuyvesant in Brooklyn. She has spent the last decade making it her dream home, painting the floors white, designing kitchen cabinets and built-in closets, and traveling the world via eBay for the best bohemian bargains. As Amhalise puts it, "What a gorgeous time to be alive. You can visit Sweden and South Africa all in a matter of minutes via blog, or buy things directly from Uzbekistan, all with the click of a mouse."

AMHALISE MORGAN
Casting director

STAR SIGN
Pisces

SPIRIT ANIMAL
Wolf

HARMONY CREE
Age 12

REBEL SPIRIT
Age 10

ON BOHEMIANISM
"It's being a free spirit and embracing travel and family. It's a home filled to the brim with love, adventure, and laughter."

OPPOSITE
In Amhalise's living room, dark woods and colorful textiles temper the gleaming white floors and walls. A large wooden star, upcycled from lath, is the focal point here. Above the star hangs a fertility mask from the Congo in the shape of a pregnant belly. Acrylic chairs, mid-century cork lamps, and a Franco Albini rattan pouf give the space a modern look, layered over rugs from Uzbekistan and home-crafted elements. When Amhalise found the leather sofa bed discarded on the sidewalk, she brought it home and had the mattress replaced and the leather cleaned. What she got was a "new" sofa.

RIGHT
Butterflies encased in frames are suspended from a branch.

BELOW
Sheepskins drape over vintage wooden patio chairs, adding a hint of the Danish modern *hygge* feel.

OPPOSITE
"My house was therapy, truly," says Amhalise. "While other moms I knew went on dates after their marriages broke up, I stayed up late checking out design blogs. If I saw something I liked, I searched for it on eBay. Nine times out of ten, I found what I was looking for at an excellent price. The nine-foot kilim on the floor in my dining area cost only ninety-nine cents!"

OPPOSITE
Amhalise designed the kitchen with the help of her contractor. The open shelving allows her to keep favorite dishes on display, like a tagine set she picked up in Tunisia. The kiwi-green and brown color palette lends an earthiness to the open space. She added a kitchen island to increase storage, as well as a dishwasher and a wine fridge.

BELOW
In the bathroom, an oval-shaped nautical window and other brass elements add a bit of natural light and shine to an otherwise dark space. Amhalise found the sink on eBay for $10 and had her contractor build the cabinet it lives in.

FOLLOWING PAGE
Amhalise coveted custom closet doors from the Brooklyn salvage yard Build It Green long before she could call them her own. "I used to visit the doors regularly," she says. "When I finally saved the money to buy them, I was elated." The tall doors set against white are striking and ground the space.

ABOVE
In Harmony's bedroom, a loft was built to maximize space. The library ladder was another curbside find. The closet doors were fashioned from a wooden screen purchased from Pier 1 Imports.

FOLLOWING PAGE
The natural light that shines into the bedroom is what sold Amhalise on the space. The white floors, walls, and ceiling increase the brightness, and on a sunny day, the room is almost blinding upon entry. The suzani bed cover and cowhide rugs were more eBay scores.

ADOPT AN IDEA

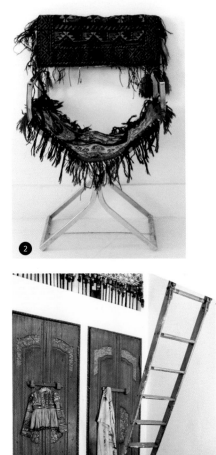

1	2	3	4
BE AN E-NOMAD	REDO A DONE-FOR CHAIR	HOW 'BOUT A RUGGER	DOORS GALORE

1

BE AN
E-NOMAD

The Turkish kilim beneath the dining table was scored on eBay for under a dollar. Sometimes it pays to search auctions with a no-reserve price on eBay.

2

REDO A
DONE-FOR CHAIR

Amhalise had this chrome director's chair with ripped suede sitting in a corner for weeks before she remembered that stack of pillow cases she had bought off eBay . . . and voilà!

3

HOW 'BOUT
A RUGGER

What's a rugger? It's a rug used as a table runner. Or at least that's what I'm calling it. Place a small rug across a table to add a pretty pop of pattern.

4

DOORS
GALORE

In both bedrooms, wooden doors break up the stark white and add a little history. Try ditching trite closet doors for salvaged or repurposed ones.

Sacha Pytka

VENICE BEACH,
CALIFORNIA

Sacha Pytka lives on Venice Beach. Really—*on* the beach, a sand-in-your-toes, salty-air, morning-yoga-with-the-Pacific-sunrise kind of on the beach. Her home sits right on the famous Venice boardwalk, where a tinted glass gate allows some privacy from the locals and tourists who walk, skate, and bike right past her front porch. Sacha has lived here for twelve years (her sister, whose home is featured on page 231, lives upstairs), and it's basically the stuff that sun-loving, bohemian California dreams are made of. "Just this morning, I saw dolphins while I was walking my dogs," she says. "As eclectic and silly as my place can be, I really love everything in it. I'm such a Cancer—a total homebody—and this place is my nest. I think you get a good sense of who I am by looking around: the closet and fashion books, family photos, vegetarian cookbooks, the collection of things on the wall, and the general plop-down-anywhere feeling here."

OPPOSITE
Nomadic bohemians gather ideas and artifacts until their homes become a visual album of their expeditions; the walls are covered with souvenirs and seashells, maps and masks, photographs and plants—each item represents an adventure. "I already use my 'future children' as an excuse to keep everything," says Sacha, "and I love that everything tells a story. Every time I do dishes, I look up at the curtain in the kitchen window and think of the fabric markets in Bali. Every time I go to bed, I look at the flag on the wall and think of our sailboat."

SACHA PYTKA
Fashion designer

STAR SIGN
Cancer

SPIRIT PLANT
Palm tree, "because it's tall and grounded, but flexible—and I love dates."

ON BOHEMIANISM
"There's the obvious that comes to mind when you think of the word 'bohemian'—fringe, embroidery, vardo wagons, and peace and love—but I think it's more about the people around me. Some work multiple jobs and others are ridiculously wealthy, but they all have a certain eye for the little details and an uncompromising sense of style that carries through everything they do. There's an appreciation for quirks and imperfections that a lot of people may not relate to."

The front patio overlooking the beach features a small garden of cacti and succulents. A daybed and fire pit await the many guests who take advantage of Sacha's home's prime location and its supremely laid-back vibe.

LEFT AND BELOW
Enter the living room from the patio through a sliding glass door and be transported into a Bedouin tent. The dreamy little living room bursts with suzanis, kilims, poufs, and plants—enough patterns to last a lifetime. The home is so layered with maps and artifacts, it is clear that Sacha has experienced many countries and cultures firsthand. During a four-year stint in Paris, Sacha journeyed to nearby North Africa. She's also traveled extensively through Europe and far-off locales like Kenya, Tanzania, Egypt, India, China, Japan, Vietnam, Indonesia, and Israel. Panama, where her boyfriend lives, is one of her favorite destinations.

ABOVE
An antique mosaic mirror hangs
with a gallery of photographs
depicting Sacha's travels with
friends and family.

OPPOSITE
The club chair was a hand-me-down
from Sacha's father. Its wonderfully
dilapidated state is partly the work
of many a family cat who used it
as a scratching post. The Tiffany
sconces were also from her childhood home.

BELOW
In the bedroom, a huge British flag that used to be on her family's sailboat covers the entire back wall. Together with a parachute cloth used as a curtain, it sets the tone for a feeling of adventure. A gold-painted ceiling makes the small room feel like a treasure chest filled with little gems of texture and color, including a punched-tin side table, indigo pillows, and a green suzani bedspread. Two classic 1970s cowrie-shell chandeliers frame the bed and a Mexican Loteria card table sits next to the bed. "Someone left that file cabinet on my doorstep ages ago," says Sacha, "and I used it to store things. One day, I got bored and painted it, glued the cards on, gave it a few coats of polyurethane, and ta-da!"

ABOVE AND FOLLOWING PAGE
Sacha's closet is like a hip boutique in Paris, only nothing is for sale and everything is a size 2. She built the shoe rack with the help of her mother; it's one of her proudest DIYs to date.

ADOPT AN IDEA

1	2	3
COVERED CUSHIONS	BUILT-INS ARE BETTER	FLAGGED DOWN

Almost all of the seat cushions at Sacha's house are covered in rugs and blankets. It is an easy way to change up the look and add a fun pop of color.

Ready-made shelves usually don't fit spaces perfectly. Built-ins maximize storage space and are an easy way to give a room more character.

Sacha's enormous flag in the bedroom packs a graphic punch. Hang a flag or other large, graphic fabric behind your bed. It is also an affordable substitute for a headboard.

NoMADic OTTOMAN

TIME: Less than one hour
ESTIMATED COST: $25
DIFFICULTY: ✱ ✱

Make two of these ottomans to use as additional seating in your living room, or make three and line them up to make a bench that sits at the foot of your bed. Put a tray on one, and this colorful ottoman can be used as a side table. This surprisingly easy project brings all those textiles you've collected on your travels out of your linen closet and into the spotlight to bring that adventurous nomadic spirit into the home.

MATERIALS

One gorgeous textile. The textile needs to be at least 30" × 30" (76 cm × 76 cm) and should be of a durable fabric. Suzani, kilim, kantha, or even regular old upholstery fabric are all good choices. If you're cutting the piece from a larger piece of fabric, think about what part of the fabric you want to use for the ottoman. I picked this piece that I found in a large pile of rags at the Pasadena City College flea market because it had square shapes in it that I thought would look fluid when placed onto a square table.

20" × 20" (50 cm × 50 cm) pillow insert. You can get pillow inserts at most fabric stores or places like West Elm or Pottery Barn; I often check stores like Ross and Marshalls for this type of thing, too.

Small side table. I used the 22" × 22" (55 cm × 55 cm) Lack side table from Ikea. It costs $8 and comes in a variety of colors. If you choose to use a table other than the Lack, make sure that the table legs can come off, and be sure to adjust the fabric and pillow measurements accordingly.

SUPPLIES

Staple gun

Staples

Fabric scissors

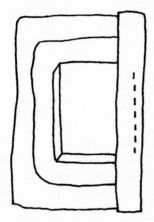
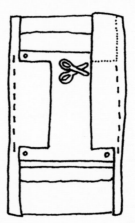
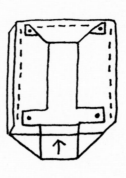
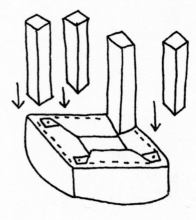

INSTRUCTIONS

1. Place the fabric facedown on the floor.

2. Center the pillow insert on the fabric.

3. Place the tabletop facedown on the pillow. Fold up one side of the fabric so that it rests flat on the back of the tabletop.

4. Making sure the fabric grain is straight, staple the fabric to the back of the tabletop at the center, then move out toward the corners, placing the staples about 2" (5 cm) apart. Pull evenly out toward the corners of the table to get any lumps out, and stop 4" (10 cm) from each corner. Repeat on the opposite side.

5. Trim the fabric down around the screw holes so that there is room to screw the table legs on.

6. Staple the fabric on the remaining two sides.

7. Finish the corners as if you were wrapping a gift. Feel free to cut and remove fabric under the corner folds, but be careful not to cut any of the fabric that will be visible at the end. Pull one side over the corner edge and secure to the tabletop underside with staples.

8. Screw the table legs onto the table and enjoy your brand-new nomadic ottoman!

FELT SUZANI-INSPIRED PILLOW

TIME: 2.5 hours

ESTIMATED COST: $10

DIFFICULTY: ✱ ✱ ✱

I love the bold graphic jolt a suzani pillow or blanket brings to a chair, couch, or bed. On a trip to Istanbul, I bought a few suzani pieces, so I can tell you from firsthand experience that suzanis are expensive. (I haggled with the merchant for 45 minutes to get him down from $350 to $250 on the cover I bought.) This project is for a pillow that provides the same visual pop of the embroidered ones, but instead of embroidery, the look is easily re-created in felt using an appliqué technique. It's also cheap and isn't too hard to make.

MATERIALS

Black felt at least 21" × 21" (53 cm × 53 cm)

Four small pieces of felt in contrasting colors. I used yellow, pink, red, and navy blue.

4' (4 m) of pom-pom trim

Polyester fiberfill. I like to use the recycled poly filling you can pick up at any craft store.

SUPPLIES

Photocopier

Scissors

Scotch tape or masking tape

Fabric scissors

Sewing pins

Needle and thread (or a sewing machine)

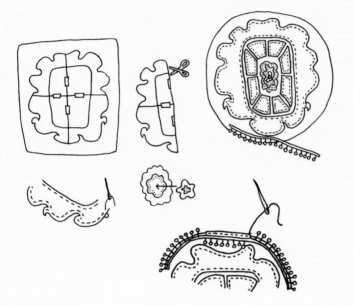

SUZANI

The word "suzani" comes from the Persian word for needle because normally suzani fabrics are embroidered in silk or cotton threads. All the suzanis I've seen include disc shapes that represent the sun, moon, and flowers, perfect for the nomadic bohemian who wants to bring the warmth of the sun, the mystery of the moon, and the sweetness of the flowers into her home.

INSTRUCTIONS

1. Enlarge Circle Template A (see page 303 for all templates) by 4 times on the photocopier and make 4 copies.

2. Cut Circle Template A from each copy and tape the pieces together to create a full circle.

3. Cut two circles from the black felt using Circle Template A.

4. Enlarge Flower Templates A and B (page 303) by 4 times and print out 2 copies of each shape.

5. Cut out all the Flower Templates and tape them together to create one large floral shape, alternating A and B. Pin the template to the yellow felt and cut the floral shape from the felt. Cut the rounded rectangle shape marked inside the floral shape from the felt (fold the felt in half to facilitate cutting).

6. Remove the paper Flower Template and pin the cut felt to the center of one of the black felt circles.

7. Stitch the yellow flower to the black circle on both the outer and inner perimeters using a straight stitch.

8. Using the Rounded Rectangle Ring Template, enlarged by 4 times on the photocopier, cut out one pink and one red rounded rectangle ring.

9. Stack the pink ring and the red ring on top of each other. Cut the rings into 8 pieces as indicated on the template.

10. Alternate the pink and red pieces inside the yellow flower on the black felt to create the inner ring. Pin and sew them into place. Save the extra pieces for a second pillow.

11. Cut out 4 more flower shapes using the Small Flower Templates, enlarged 4 times, in 4 different colors. Pin the smallest one to the next-smallest one and sew it in place. Then pin those two to the

next-largest one and sew them together. Continue until all of the flowers are sewn to one another, always sewing around the perimeter of the flowers. Then sew the largest flower to the black felt so that all the flowers are attached to the piece at its center.

12. Sew the pom-pom trim to the edge of the black circle.

13. Put the two black circles face-to-face (tuck the pom-poms to the inside) and sew around the perimeter with a small seam allowance until the pillow is four-fifths of the way closed. Turn the pillow right-side out.

14. Stuff the pillow with the fiberfill.

15. Stitch the opening closed by hand. Now toss your new pillow onto your bed, sofa, or favorite chair to add that sunny burst of suzani.

The Romantic Bohemian

The romantic bohemian often trades in contrasts, between the natural and the supernatural, the familiar and the exotic, the narrative and the poetic. Objects are relics. The home is a theatrical space, full of dramatic moments, music, and circuslike quirks. The arts flirt with the sciences. Old pianos, binoculars, and beakers play the role of both sculpture and instrument. These homes are glamorous and faded, considered and whimsical, worldly and otherworldly.

THE Romantic

BOHEMIAN

Erica Tanov
&
Steven Emerson

BERKELEY, CALIFORNIA

Nestled among the tall pines in the Berkeley Hills, Erica Tanov's 1926 Mediterranean-style home exemplifies the romantic bohemian's contradictions. It is lovingly cared for, but acknowledges the beauty of decay. It feels both foreign and familiar, like home but also like an adventure. De Gournay wallpapers blend seamlessly with her children's artwork. There is drama and romance, but also a quiet playfulness. Not just a home for her and for family, it's also a theater, design studio, and concert hall. "Perhaps I am channeling Picasso's French Villa La Californie. I love the haphazard, artistic, chaotic, crumbling grandeur."

ERICA TANOV
Interior design consultant and designer of clothing and homewares for her boutique, Erica Tanov

STAR SIGN
Sagittarius

SPIRIT ANIMAL
Deer

STEVEN EMERSON
Musician, composer

ISABELLE
Age 17

HUGO
Age 12

ON BOHEMIANISM
"Free thinking, free spirited, untethered, stylistically hippie with a touch of glamour."

OPPOSITE
The living room is mutable and informal. A Danish-Modern sofa is surrounded by several small Moroccan tables that can be moved around the room depending on the circumstances of the day. The result is a living room that suits everyone's needs.

OPPOSITE
The hallway is rich with pattern and art: The wallpaper is from Osborne and Little and the portrait is by her daughter Isabelle.

RIGHT
A Moroccan Beni Ourain rug adds texture to a large, airy living room. A shawl is draped neatly over the mid-century chair for a playful pink accent. The round burl-wood stool doubles as a table.

BELOW
Quirky collections of family photos, children's artwork, and mementos from their travels fill the built-in bookshelves.

ABOVE
On special occasions, the bottom floor of this three-story house is converted from Erica's husband Steven's studio into a performance space.

OPPOSITE
Music permeates the home. Steven is a musician and composer, and this piano was inherited from his great-aunt and great-uncle. On the wall hangs a portrait of a girl by Elodia Muzzi (Erica's late cousin) and two collage paintings by Alexander Kori Girard.

LEFT
Built-in shelves from previous owners were torn out, and their splotchy legacy on the wall harmonizes with the vintage pieces in the surrounding decor. The mid-century Chinoiserie cabinet doubles as a bar.

ABOVE
In the sitting room, a kantha quilt and an eclectic array of throw pillows cover a single bed. A Moroccan lantern with red glass casts a pretty design on the ceiling and lends a warm, pinkish glow to the entire room.

ABOVE
Prints, paintings, and photographs form a kind of gallery above a mid-century sofa adorned in bright pillows with pom-pom trims. "Textiles are my weakness," says Erica.

OPPOSITE
Erica's studio used to be an outdoor patio. She added windows and a roof, creating an indoor-outdoor space that is quite distinct from the rest of the house. The walls are full of windows and mirrors, making this sunny spot perfect for conjuring up new design schemes.

LEFT
The bedroom is the ultimate space in this home. Striking hand-painted De Gournay wallpaper that is now aging in the most wonderful way was Erica's most extravagant purchase for the home. A transparent table lamp provides height and light without blocking too much of the gorgeous wallpaper.

ABOVE
The Chinese floral motif reappears on a bedside lamp, offering a variation on the wallpaper theme without competing with it.

FOLLOWING PAGE
A sophisticated Chinese-style black dresser is set against what used to be an exterior wall that is now adorned with inspiring doodles and a collection of pages torn out of magazines.

ADOPT AN IDEA

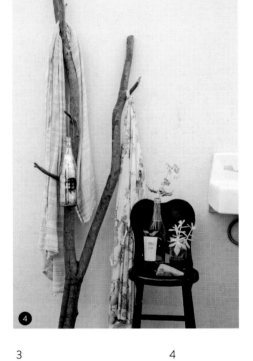

1	2	3	4
PAINT IT BLACK	TWICE AS NICE, HALF THE PRICE	UNITED COLORS OF GLASSWARE	BRANCH OUT

1 — PAINT IT BLACK

Erica's dressers are all glossy and black. If you have an old dresser that needs a little love, paint it black. Add brass hardware for shine and let it patina.

2 — TWICE AS NICE, HALF THE PRICE

When you have a statement lamp as great as this one, it's nice to see double. Use mirrors to reflect your favorite lamps to get twice the light and twice the lamp.

3 — UNITED COLORS OF GLASSWARE

Choose themes that unite collections. Gold accents are what give this eclectic group of glasses a cohesive, collected look.

4 — BRANCH OUT

A large branch makes a great towel rack in the bathroom.

Jared Frank

LOS ANGELES, CALIFORNIA

The Silver Lake home of Jared Frank has all of the beauty, darkness, and surreality of a circus. Murals come to life in playful acts of trompe l'oeil. Masks—some jolly and others terrifying—peer out from shadows cast by theatrical lighting. Spirits animate the space, evoking the glories and tragedies of past lives. Relationships with these spirits play a starring role in this home. The most prominent spirit is that of a former tenant, the late Lance Klemm, whose fresco murals linger on the walls, floors, and ceilings. "I was primarily inspired by Klemm's frescos," says Jared. "My decoration throughout is a response to his ornament. His playful attitude, dramatic theatricality, and sense of history inform all my choices."

JARED FRANK
Interior designer, set designer, and founder of Topsy Design

STAR SIGN
Cancer

SPIRIT ANIMAL
Topsy the elephant. "She was electrocuted by Thomas Edison in 1903 at Coney Island in an attempt to discredit Westinghouse's alternating current. The short film, which was shown across the United States, was the first widely seen recording of a creature's death. I've named my company Topsy Design in memory of her."

ON BOHEMIANISM
"Narrative mystery is what I love most about living here. Many artists leave their work on the easel, in the studio. But a bohemian lives his or her art daily. They bring their creative spirit home."

OPPOSITE The foyer is the most dramatic space in the home and functions as a spiritual palate cleanser—forget the humdrum banality of the world outside and welcome to a world of mystery and magic. Like a fortune-teller's tent, the light here is dark and red. It feels more like a movie set than a home, except for the shoes, mail, and umbrellas.

BELOW

A large "Topsy" sign illuminates a collection of papier-mâché masks. The bearded mask represents Goliath and was used in a ceremony held by the Independent Order of Odd Fellows reenacting the biblical story of David and Goliath. "One of the things I like best about ceremonial artifacts from secret orders is that one can never know the full story of the objects," says Jared. "As these lodges go the way of history, their secrets go with them. The objects left behind can be appreciated for their intrinsic aesthetic qualities as well as their obscured narratives of use."

RIGHT AND FOLLOWING PAGE

In the living room, the atmosphere becomes less theatrical and more period: "While decorating this house, I was particularly drawn to the period after industrialization but before World War II," says Jared. "But in my work as a whole, I'm an equal-opportunity history buff." A mid-century Falcon chair sits under a turn-of-the-century gramophone horn, repurposed as a pendant lamp. A stack of vintage suitcases is used as a coffee table. A collection of old English street signs rests on a floor exquisitely painted by the former tenant, Lance Klemm. "I never met Lance before he passed, but he speaks to me daily through his art. In one place, above an archway in my living room, I kept a note he wrote: *Carpe Diem*."

ABOVE
A cutting board rests on three pedestals to create a bricolage side table.

RIGHT
"When I design for clients, everything is methodically planned out in collaboration," says Jared. "The biggest difference about decorating for myself is that rooms reveal themselves only over a period of time. This allows for both serendipity and continuous revision, a luxury that makes up for my much tighter budget."

FOLLOWING SPREAD
The particular way objects and furniture are arranged suggests symbolic relationships between them and shape the way people relate to them and to each other. In Jared's home, especially the dining room, the placement of objects is deliberate, precisely in order to create particular narratives. "In my home," he says, "the way objects are displayed and the relationships among them are just as important as the objects themselves."

ABOVE AND OPPOSITE
Strings of beads adorn the entryway to the kitchen, where the linoleum Jared installed adds a playful 1950s vibe. A built-in bench sits behind a vintage industrial-style collapsible table. The miniature kilim and embroidered pillows on the bench were purchased on eBay.

Moss-green built-in shelves with quirky details give the kitchen a vaguely Tuscan feel. They were built by Lance but look as though they might have been found at a salvage yard. The narrow shelves take up very little space but go all the way up to the ceiling, making them a perfect small-kitchen storage solution.

FOLLOWING PAGE
The charming patio's weathered details and succulent garden evoke the Mediterranean.

ADOPT AN IDEA

1	2	3	4
PAPER UMBRELLAMPS	**YOU GOT THE LOOK**	**NAILED IT**	**NICE BULBS**

In the entryway, Jared rigged paper umbrellas to lamp cages from a hardware store. The result is visually eye-catching and enhances the mood lighting.

The former owner glued white-painted shells onto the fireplace mantel, which Jared decided to keep.

Who says curtains need to hang on curtain rods? I love Jared's solution of hanging curtains onto nails and twisting them back in a romantic gesture.

The filament light bulbs in the chandelier may be pricier than regular bulbs, but they add to the romance and charm of the space.

Arielle Pytka

VENICE BEACH, CALIFORNIA

Arielle Pytka has called this loftlike space on Venice Beach home since high school, when she lived here with her father. He eventually moved out, but Arielle stayed to make this place a canvas for her sophisticated and eclectic tastes (her sister lives downstairs, see page 187). Here, dark meets dreamy and the elaborate meets the scattered. It's home, but it's also a playground for creative pursuits: Upstairs is a darkroom and downstairs is a music room where jam sessions go late into the night. "How can I describe my home? It's a perfect mess!"

ARIELLE PYTKA
Artist

STAR SIGN
Pisces

SPIRIT ANIMAL
Arabian horse

ON BOHEMIANISM
"Paris in the 1920s."

OPPOSITE AND FOLLOWING PAGE
Arielle's taste is sophisticated for someone so young. The Victorian aquarium purchased at Blackman Cruz was one of her own discoveries, and it was also her idea to fill it with potted cacti. The fantastic result is a major statement piece. Several elements of the living room, like the gothic candlesticks on the coffin or the throne at the wooden slab table, give it a dark and fantastical—almost medieval—feeling. It's not always clear which artifacts are holdovers from her father's reign and which Arielle brought in herself.

ABOVE
The shucking leather club chair
(its twin lives in sister Sacha's
apartment downstairs) is in front
of a gallery wall full of black-and-
white photos, many of which Arielle
developed in her own darkroom
upstairs.

ABOVE
A vintage safe functions as a side table.

RIGHT
An impressive collection of vintage books fills the shelves, adding a sense of color and history.

OPPOSITE
An enormous floral patterned rug Arielle inherited from her parents covers the unfinished wooden stairs that lead up to the bedroom. Squished into the narrow stairway, it feels simultaneously bizarre and brilliant. "I randomly put it there one day and just left it there," says Arielle. "I can't believe no one has ever fallen on it!"

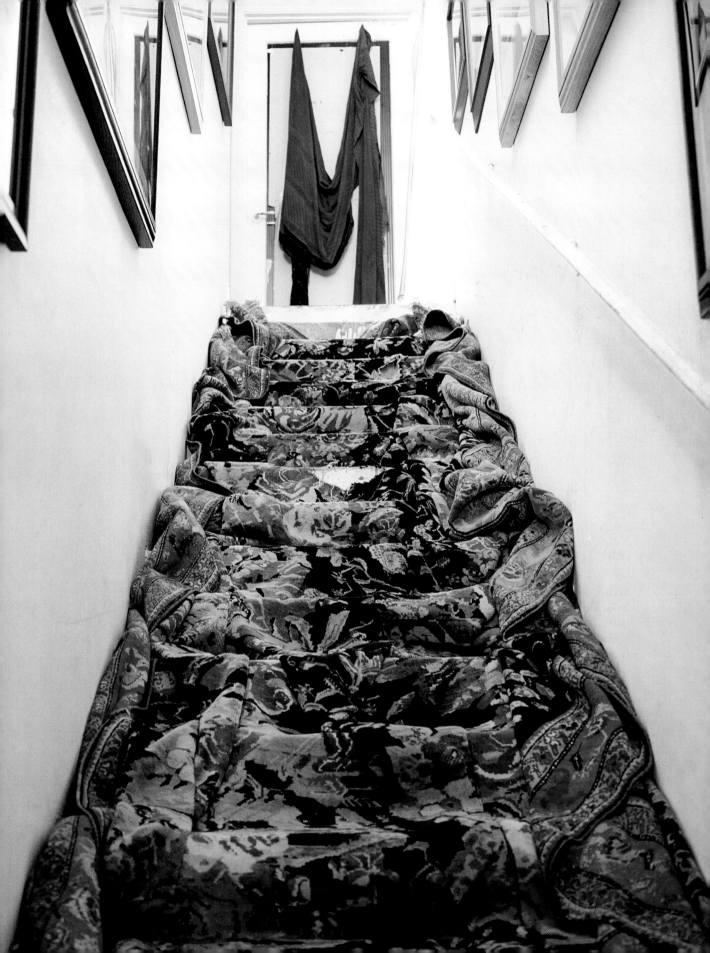

OPPOSITE, RIGHT, AND FOLLOWING PAGE
Aside from the pristine white bed, everything about the bedroom feels weathered and ancient. A large vintage lace tablecloth found at the Rose Bowl flea market in Pasadena is draped casually over the window. Two art nouveau–style floor lamps look like they were found in Paris. Punched-tin frames hold childhood photos of Arielle and her sister Sacha. Several dream catchers hang above Arielle's bed. Her mother made her favorite one using hair from the tail of her favorite childhood horse, Silver, a purebred Arabian.

ADOPT AN IDEA

1
RUGGED
GOOD LOOKS

While I may have cut to fit the rug on the stairs of my home, and nailed/glued it in place, I love the idea of covering a stairway with a beautiful vintage rug.

2
A STENCILED
WELCOME

Arielle used a stencil to paint a "mat" on the floor outside the bedroom. I think this trompe l'oeil detail is a fun idea. Put one inside the entryway of a home.

3
AGE OF
AQUARIUM

My favorite element of Arielle's home is the Victorian aquarium turned terrarium. With some salvaged hardware, an old aquarium, and a hot glue gun, a similar "wow" look can be achieved in any home.

FAUX STAINED GLASS
WINDOW

TIME: 4 hours

ESTIMATED COST: $40

DIFFICULTY: ✳

WITH NATALIE GLUCK MITCHELL

I love stained glass not only for the colors it brings into a room but also for the romantic colored light that it produces. This faux stained glass window can simply be decorative, or it can be functional if placed in a window. Alternatively, the same technique could be applied directly to a window. Use it in a small room to lend a warm glow to the space.

MATERIALS

Old window. I found this one discarded on the curb, but you can find them at salvage yards and flea markets.

Lighting gel sheets in various colors. I used lighting gels (from Guitar Center) and spray adhesive, but transparent vinyl sheeting with adhesive is available on eBay from Paper Street Plastics. You will still outline and cut the shapes the same way, but they will be applied like stickers—no glue needed.

Repositionable spray adhesive

Screw hooks or S hooks

SUPPLIES

Measuring tape

Pencil

Poster board—at least the same size as the window

Cutting mat

Ruler or stencils

Craft knife

Thin, strong rope (at least a couple of yards)

Hammer and nails

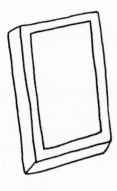
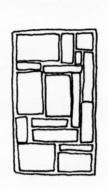
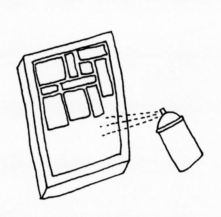
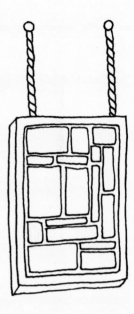

INSTRUCTIONS

1. Measure the glass area you're going to cover on your window. Draw a rectangle exactly that size on the poster board so that you can lay out your design before adhering it to the window.

2. Lay the gel sheets on the mat and, using a ruler or stencil, cut the desired shapes for the design. I used rectangles and squares to fill the entire space.

3. As you go, lay the shapes on the poster board (position this near the window for easy transfer). If you're trying to re-create this specific design, it is helpful to loosely keep track of measurements so that you can complete the whole puzzle.

4. Once you're happy with your design, following the directions on the spray adhesive, cover the top half of the window and work quickly to adhere one piece of gel at a time. Then complete the lower half.

5. Place the stained glass window in the desired location. You can arrange it like art on a console to complete a vignette or hang it in front of a window. If you do wish to hang your window, attach the screw hooks or S-hooks to the top of the wooden window frame a couple of inches from the outer edges. Cut two pieces of rope the right length for where you want to hang the window (don't forget to add a few inches of rope on both ends so that you have enough space to tie knots). Thread the rope through one hook and tie securely. Repeat on the other side. Tie sturdy loops on the other ends of the rope. Measure the distance between the two hooks. Use that measurement to place nails or screws in the wall, depending on the type of wall you have. Place rope loops on the nails or screws to hang the window in place.

6. Enjoy the new colorful view!

PYRITE PLANTERS

TIME: 1 hour, plus drying time
ESTIMATED COST: $25
DIFFICULTY: *

Pyrite is said to be a protective stone that shields against negative energies—perfect for the home of the romantic bohemian, yes? These planters bring on the healing energy and the glam. Replicate the idea for vases, candleholders, and frames, too.

MATERIALS

2 pounds (1 kg) marble-size pyrite pieces. I got mine on eBay using the search term "pyrite lot"; on most sites, I found it cost around $10 a pound ($4.50/kg). I used less than 2 pounds (1 kg) for this project.

2 small terra-cotta planters—available at your local garden center and most craft stores

Loctite Go2 Glue

Potting soil for succulents

A collection of succulents

SUPPLIES

Towel

Hammer

Protective goggles

INSTRUCTIONS

1. If any pyrite pieces are too large, you can wrap them in a towel, place on a cement surface, and gently hammer into smaller pieces. Aim for marble-size pieces—you don't want any of the pieces to be too heavy. Be sure to wear protective goggles when you do this.

2. With the terra-cotta pots sitting upright, start gluing the pyrite pieces to the bottom edge of the planters, all the way around. Use generous amounts of glue. Let the glue set for about half an hour, and then continue with the second row. Think of this as a puzzle, fitting the pieces together, filling any negative space. Rotate the pieces so that the flattest edge of the pyrite is up against the planter, and place the pyrite pieces as close together as possible.

3. Continue to glue the pyrite pieces onto the planter until you reach the top. Let the glue set for 48 hours.

4. Fill the planters with potting soil and a plant with shallow roots, like a succulent. Enjoy all the positive vibes you just ushered into your home!

The Maximal Bohemian

Maximal bohemians mean no offense toward their quiet cousin, minimalism, but whereas the minimalist strips things to the bare bones, maximal bohemians surround themselves with eye candy. Every surface of the home is abundant with art—the walls are canvases to be patterned, painted, and planted; floors and furniture are buried in pillows and textiles; and shelves are filled with books and beloved objects. With a strong disregard for quaint notions like everything must match or line up, the maximal bohemian loves to decorate wild.

THE Maximal

BOHEMIAN

Louise Ingalls Sturges & Tyler Hammond Brodie

NEW YORK, NEW YORK

Since 1916, Manhattan's West Village has been known as Little Bohemia. It is hard to imagine a home that exemplifies that spirit more than Louise and Tyler's Casa de Casual Rainbow. For starters, its rainbow-colored facade announces the theme that runs throughout the interior, where a red-orange-yellow-green-blue-indigo-violet (ROYGBIV) scheme imposes a kind of order on a wealth of art, artifacts, fabrics, and furnishings. Disco balls and prisms compound the effect, reflecting and refracting rainbows throughout, making this home a maximal trip-out salon. Says Louise about the place: "I had the idea to do a gradient paint job on the back of the house, and Tyler responded with, 'Why wouldn't we just paint it rainbow?' to which I replied, 'Will you marry me again?!'"

OPPOSITE AND FOLLOWING SPREAD
Louise and Tyler's living room is a kaleidoscopic wonderland. The eye bounces from image to object, from rug to textile, and never ceases to find something crazy, bright, bold, or downright spectacular to look at. Two sofas frame a fireplace full of candles. Two coffee tables, one mid-century modern and one repurposed old trunk, provide places to kick up one's feet. "Our home is cozy and bright," says Louise. "It's full of happy things that we've collected from our travels and families, and sourced from thrift stores and Moroccan souks. We both still have furniture and clothes from our freshman year in college, so we're certainly collectors. But there is a fine line between collecting and hoarding, and as far as I'm concerned, the line is drawn at organization."

LOUISE INGALLS STURGES
Artist

STAR SIGN
Libra

SPIRIT ANIMAL
Coyote, "my actual Native American spirit animal, but birds come up a lot in my tarot practice—so I'd say somewhere between the earth and the sky. Rainbow is my nature spirit, full of color and atmosphere and water and sunshine."

TYLER HAMMOND BRODIE
Artist, music and film producer

STAR SIGN
Cancer

SPIRIT ANIMAL
"Somewhere between Tigger, a turtle, and a peacock."

ON BOHEMIANISM
"We're gypsy travelers, constantly accumulating and ever evolving. We're totally creative colorful hippies who collect stuff and love to travel, and I think by some loose definition that puts us under the bohemian umbrella."

OPPOSITE AND ABOVE
Collections of objects, books, and even photographs are organized into the ROYGBIV spectrum. "We hold on to objects and maybe thus archive the memories," says Louise. "But we do it all in the full spectrum of the rainbow."

ABOVE
Two desks in the back of the room make a working space that most couples living in a large five-story townhouse would not be willing to share. The intimacy of these newlyweds is on display in every colorful corner in their home.

OPPOSITE
A fireplace mantel in the dining room is surrounded by art that Louise purchased mostly from her brother's art gallery, Plane Space.

ABOVE
A vintage Lucite sofa is buried in pillows of different shades and patterns. Moroccan floor pillows mix with shaggy accent pillows, just one of the many instances where Louise mixes modern design elements with vintage Moroccan textiles.

OPPOSITE
The half circle of floor-to-ceiling windows define a lounge area that overlooks the backyard. A gallery wall, bright pink kilim rug, and enormous disco ball, used as a footrest, enchant this comfortable niche. However, the arrangement is not static, as items often get shuffled around and reorganized. "Tyler says our home is a work in progress, which is absolutely true," explains Louise. "It is a space in constant flux—a reflection of us as people and as artists, I suppose."

ABOVE
Though bursting with joyful color and pattern, the bedroom maintains an atmosphere of comfort and relaxation. Dream catchers in every shade dance on the ceiling. Vintage Moroccan and modern Scandinavian textiles articulate the bed. The headboard is simply a large piece of Marimekko fabric pinned to the wall. "Our home is a mish-mash, a palimpsest of our lives," says Louise.

OPPOSITE
The master bathroom doubles as Louise's closet. A plant stand is used to hold shoes, and a vintage caddy from Kartell is used to hold and display Louise's jewelry collection. Having spent many years in Santa Fe, New Mexico, she has amassed a striking collection of turquoise jewelry pieces. "I can find beautiful colorful things anywhere. This goes for photography, clothes, jewelry, and mixed-media materials. My influences range from mid-century modern design—modular units, Plexiglas, and primary color fields—to Native American arts and crafts."

FOLLOWING SPREAD
On the top floor is Louise's light-filled artist's studio. The Empire State Building is visible from the rooftop.

PAGE 260
A spectrum of scarves are stored and displayed on the bannister that leads up to the bedroom.

ADOPT AN IDEA

1
DON'T BE
BORING

While you don't have to
paint your entire home like
a rainbow to add pizzazz,
a colorful trim or even a
brightly painted front door
can add a jolt of personality.

2
PARTY
OVER HERE

Hang disco balls in rooms
and prisms on windows to
add reflections of rainbows
and glimmering spots of
lights dancing around your
home.

3
WALL
FABRIC

Use fabric on walls as
though it were wallpaper.
This Marimekko fabric was
installed with a staple gun.

4
BLESS
THIS MESS

Use *ojos de dios* ("god's
eyes") in the windows to
add color and obscure the
view into the home.

Adam Pogue

LOS ANGELES, CALIFORNIA

The coolness of this concrete, L-shaped downtown loft is warmed by years of collecting, tinkering, patching, playing, and propagating. Adam Pogue is one of those rare creatives who has a great eye and a great hand. Textiles have been cut, painted, tied, and dyed to create partitions, headboards, sofa coverings, and art. Plants twist and flop and multiply. It's the kind of environment that can only be crafted with time, adding layer upon layer—there is no planning a home like this or throwing it together. It's a constant work in progress, yet perfect just the way it is at every step of the way. "I have put my hand on almost everything in my space," says Adam.

ADAM POGUE
Works for FREECITY

STAR SIGN
Leo

SPIRIT PLANT
Mother of Thousands,
"cause she does what she wants!"

ON BOHEMIANISM
"A bohemian is someone who does their own thing. If you don't have it, make it. Or make it work for you."

OPPOSITE
Adam's cat, Sissy, watches the concrete jungle of downtown Los Angeles from the comfort of their indoor jungle.

OPPOSITE
Just outside the massive loft windows, the bustle of downtown Los Angeles is in full swing. But inside, filtering the clamor and impurity of this commercial and industrial environment, is a wall of plants: They are perched on a window bench, hanging from water pipes, or simply sitting on the floor. Rubber trees, fiddle-leaf figs, succulents, and philodendrons—they're all wild and unkempt, just doing their thing.

BELOW
The entrance leads directly into an open, modern kitchen. A wild plant greets guests from a DIY wall pocket. A small backsplash of twelve tiles adds a bit of pattern.

BELOW

Adam's patchwork sofa is the pièce de résistance of the living room. Sofas are big investments, and it can be tough to find a great one that is affordable, and custom upholstery jobs can be pricey. The solution? Do it yourself! "The couch was the first large piece of furniture I bought on my own," recalls Adam. "It was in the 'as-is' section of a local furniture store for $150. After a few years, the light upholstery wasn't looking so great, and professional reupholstery wasn't in my budget. After a work trip to Japan, I fell in love with boro textiles. I have been hand-sewing for a while, so it was natural for me to just start sewing these scraps directly onto the upholstery on the couch. It took close to a full year to cover it. I am actually almost done sewing another layer on top of this one. I'm re-covering the re-covering."

OPPOSITE

Many loft dwellers love taking advantage of their large open spaces but miss having the privacy that walls and doors afford. Adam's solution is equal parts pretty and practical. He bought several cheap white tab-top curtains from Ikea and sewed them together to create one large panel, which he hung over a cord suspended across the room. The end result needed some color, however, so he dip-dyed the fabric in a mix of red and magenta Rit dye, then added another layer of navy and denim dye. "Even though there are no walls, it feels like a separate room when the curtain is closed," says Adam.

Growing succulents from clippings is an easy, fun, and affordable alternative to buying grown plants. Carefully pluck a leaf off of the stem of the plant and let it sit for three days on a plate, in bright but indirect light so that the end can dry out and callous over. Then place it on top of a pot of well-drained potting soil and wait a few weeks until you notice tiny roots and baby leaves sprouting from the end of the leaf. "Once the leaf has grown roots, explains Adam, "then plant that baby and watch it grow."

PREVIOUS SPREAD

Some walls are not drillable so hanging art, shelves, TVs, or anything on them is not an option. Adam's solution for these walls was to paint an abstract geometric mural directly onto the wall. You get the art without the holes in the wall. "For the mural, I knew I wanted a houselike shape in the center and the rest kind of came out of that. I didn't do a lot of preplanning. It came to me as I went. I mixed and used house paints and acrylic paints that I already had in the house."

OPPOSITE

The bedroom area behind Adam's curtain is defined by Behr's Marine Magic paint. The cool color creates a relaxing backdrop for pops of color provided by his green plants, blue blankets, orange stool, and headboard made of multicolored rags. Moroccan rag rugs, also known as boucherouite rugs, come with a pretty heavy price, but Adam's is completely DIY. "When I was little, my sister-in-law used to make these rugs out of old rags," Adam recalls. "They were really simple: just rows of knots linked to each other. We had been doing dye samples on fleece at work, and I ended up taking home all this great dyed fleece. To make a long story short, the piece above my bed is my attempt at a giant fleece knot rug!"

FOLLOWING PAGE

Adam's hand-painted mural is the backdrop for his budding fiddle-leaf fig and a handmade brass and fabric table lamp.

ADOPT AN IDEA

1
A BRIGHT
IDEA

Ceramic planters are cleverly converted into bedside lamps by turning
the pots upside down and installing
a simple lighting kit. Adam painted
the pots in a high-gloss sign paint and
mounted them to the wall. Imagine
the same concept with smaller pots,
and painted gold—the possibilities are
endless!

2
BACKSPLASH
IN A FLASH

Buy a few expensive patterned tiles
to use as a small backsplash, so you
achieve the effect without spending
your whole paycheck.

3
DIY
PLANTERS

Planters can be made from almost
anything. I love the way Adam uses
fabric to hold plants. Whether you
cover a pot in a felt bucket or hang
a plant on the wall in an old military
bag, get creative with what you keep
your plants in.

Justina Blakeney & Jason Rosencrantz

LOS ANGELES, CALIFORNIA

My own home, nestled in a surprisingly green residential pocket on Crown Hill, just blocks from downtown Los Angeles, is not only the place where my husband and I raise our daughter but also my office, workshop, and photo studio. Our ecologically minded landlord equipped the home with solar panels and a gray water system, but we layered on the pattern, plants, and personality that turned this bungalow into what we call the "jungalow."

OPPOSITE
A wooden cabinet stands at the entryway to our jungalow. Plants spill forth from some of the drawers, while the rest are full of crafting supplies, old postcards, and family photos. A vintage mannequin found abandoned in the street greets visitors and occasionally functions as a rack for hats and coats.

FOLLOWING SPREAD
A warm orange theme unifies a living room that is otherwise exploding with color. A sectional sofabed remains in the open position to instill a laid-back loungey feel. It's covered with a round Greek flokati rug purchased at World Market and a host of throw pillows. Above the sofa, a playful art installation holds pieces picked up in travels around the world.

JUSTINA BLAKENEY
Designer, blogger, stylist, author

STAR SIGN
Aries

SPIRIT ANIMAL
Panda bear

JASON ROSENCRANTZ
Stay-at-home dad,
jack-of-some-trades

STAR SIGN
Libra

SPIRIT PLANT
Fern

IDA
Age 2

ON BOHEMIANISM
"A life of adventure and creativity and an insatiable need to create and surround oneself with the wild and the beautiful."

PREVIOUS SPREAD
The front yard is a riot of color and pattern that come together to create an outdoor living room where we regularly chill out and entertain guests.

LEFT AND OPPOSITE
Opposite the fireplace, a mid-century-style shelving unit covers almost the entire wall. I enjoy styling it with books, plants, sculptures, and artwork, or anything that is inspiring me at the moment. Every season, I switch it up and put new things on display.

TEN TIPS FOR STYLING A BOOKSHELF

1. Spacing and placement is the difference between a tableau looking collected or cluttered. Try grouping items together in mini-collections and place them strategically.

2. Create visual balance by contrasting shapes and sizes. If you have a stack of square objects, for example, try placing something that is round or amorphous on top. If you are working with items of varying heights, place taller items in the back and smaller items in front.

3. Repetition can be good: Place two or more identical vases in a row, to give the eye a break.

4. Remember the power of threes: Placing objects in groups of three tends to be visually pleasing.

5. Generally speaking, organize books by color (put similar colors together) and size (from largest on bottom to smallest on top.

6. On the same shelf, place organized stacks of books horizontally and others standing vertically.

7. Place art among the books. Use paintings or even outward-facing books (so the covers are visible) to fill in negative space.

8. Add plants and/or flowers to enliven the look of the shelves. Flowers and plants breathe life into everything.

9. Add a bit of bling. My favorite bling tends to vary; at present time, brass is my bling of choice. But any metallic, crystal, or even glass can provide the desired sparkle to any vignette.

10. Have fun and experiment. Much of the time, styling shelves is just about moving things around until everything looks and feels right.

ABOVE
In the kitchen, I wanted to create a greenhouse vibe. For paint, we settled on Mint Sprig by Behr, but we left most of it white so as not to overwhelm the eyes. A curtain of plants hangs over one window. A ceramic Talavera cattle skull picked up in Baja, California, doubles as a vase. A vintage brass pendant lamp, a white pedestal table from CB2, and a set of Verner Panton S chairs inherited from Grandma Bette give the space a modern feel. An agave plant from the backyard grows in a simple glass jar on the kitchen table.

OPPOSITE
My favorite kitchen detail is our shelved window. The collection of glass, porcelain, flowers, and plants on display here is relatively spare (for this maximalist, anyway) in order to allow the natural light to shine through.

OPPOSITE AND ABOVE
With its high wooden ceilings and oddly shaped windows, our bedroom has great bones, as they say, so it was easy to work with. The simple Ikea storage bed is made beautiful by adding a Moroccan wedding blanket and contrasting pillows. Instead of a traditional headboard, I used an unsigned painted canvas I found at a thrift shop. From the tops of the windows toward the center of the ceiling, I've draped two Turkish towels, and

at the apex hangs a pom-pom lantern I found at a Swiss *hiob* ("thrift shop"). I keep my prettiest clothing on matching hangers on an exposed floating rack, partially because of lack of storage, but also to display more pattern and color. A mini-tower of reclaimed windows is mounted on the wall to add visual interest without too much heaviness.

I designed a mid-century-style windowseat to fit a niche in our bedroom and had it built by

the same craftsman who built the wall unit in the living room. It does triple duty as storage, desk, and window bench. It has also been used as a changing table, a craft table, and, inevitably, a cat bed. The hanging planter is my own design and is another collaboration with local craftspeople.

LEFT
I obtained a mid-century six-drawer dresser with slim legs at a bargain price because someone had painted it white, thereby decreasing its value. I wanted a white dresser anyway, so it was a perfect match!

BELOW
Odds and ends are gathered onto a wooden tray to keep the dresser from looking messy.

OPPOSITE
Facing the bed is a vintage dresser found at Junk, a shop in Brooklyn, New York. I've painted it many colors over the years; right now it's turquoise. I painted a strip of wall behind the dresser in the same color, which gives the impression that it's built in.

FOLLOWING PAGE
Ida's room—formerly my walk-in closet!—is the perfect size for making building blocks, piecing together puzzles, flipping through books, or taking a nap. When I was eight months pregnant, I spent a "nesting day" upholstering the back wall in a simple striped fabric to provide a little cushion and a pop of pattern.

ADOPT AN IDEA

1	2	3	4
SHAPE UP	PLANTEL	MONOCHROMOSAIC	SUCCULENT STORAGE

Paint a shape, for instance a blue rectangle, on the wall and hang a shelf painted to match. The result is an instant art installation where you can store and display your favorite objects.

Mantels over fireplaces are often skinny, so styling them can be tricky. My solution? Cover them with small potted plants, and switch them out seasonally.

Part of the beauty of mosaic emerges from the array of colors and shapes, but painting a mosaic a single color emphasizes the great textures. Try this if you already have a lot of colors in a space.

Line a drawer with plastic (garbage bags) and fill them half-full with pebbles, then fill the rest with potting soil. Use plants that don't need a lot of water, like succulents or cacti, and make sure they get lots of sunlight. Water the plants sparingly, and only when the soil is dry.

KUBA CLOCK

TIME: Less than a half hour

ESTIMATED COST: $7

DIFFICULTY: *

The maximal bohemian uses fabric everywhere— we make rag rugs from leftover felt, use Marimekko fabric like wallpaper, and cover every upholstered surface in our homes with layers of fabric to add pattern and color. This clock is an easy way to bring a pop of pattern into the home, even if you're not a maximalist. I love this project because it's so fast and easy; it's functional and easily customizable to fit your taste. I used a piece of tie-dyed raffia kuba cloth from the Democratic Republic of the Congo. Another reason I love this project is that it gives me a chance to use this small piece of beautiful fabric I didn't know what to do with.

MATERIALS

1 scrap of amazing fabric at least 11½" × 14" (29 cm × 35.5 cm)

1 stretched canvas 8½" × 11" (21.5 cm × 28 cm)

1 clock mechanism. I chose white so that the color would stand out against the dark fabric. I bought it on eBay for $3, but mechanisms can be purchased at most craft stores.

SUPPLIES

Scissors

Staple gun

Staples

Tape measure

Pen

Hammer

Nail

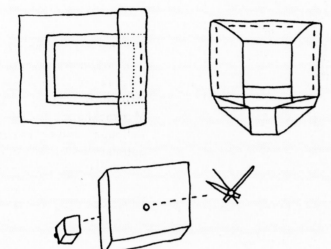

INSTRUCTIONS

1. Before you cut the fabric, be sure to think about the pattern you're working with and which part of the pattern you want on the canvas and where. Then cut the fabric so that it is 3" (7.5 cm) larger than the canvas on all sides.

2. Lay the fabric facedown on a clean, flat surface and center the canvas facedown on top of it. Make sure the fabric grain is straight.

3. Fold up one side of the fabric so that it rests flat on the back of the canvas.

4. Staple the fabric to the back of the canvas frame at the center of one edge, then move out toward the corners. Place the staples about 1" (2.5 cm) apart, stapling a little at a time. Pull evenly out toward the corners to get any lumps out, stopping 2" (5 cm) from each corner. Staple the opposite side, then repeat with the remaining two sides.

5. Finish the corners as if you were wrapping a gift. Feel free to cut and remove any fabric under the corner folds, but be careful not to cut any of the fabric that will be visible at the end. Pull one side over the corner edge and secure to the canvas frame with staples.

6. Decide where you want the clock mechanism to be placed on the canvas. I like the look of the clock being off-center, to add a bit of quirk. Measure the clock mechanism to make sure that the hands don't go past the canvas frame, and mark the spot on the canvas.

7. Using the tip of the scissors, carefully puncture a tiny hole through the fabric and canvas. Follow the clock mechanism instructions to install the hands on the front of the canvas and the battery mechanism on the back.

8. Hammer the nail into the wall at the desired location and hang the clock. Now enjoy the ticktock of the cutest time teller on the block!

KUBA

Kuba cloth from the Democratic Republic of the Congo is woven from the fibers of the *Raphia vinifera* palm. First, the fibers are gathered and prepped, then they're woven into cloth on a single-heddle loom. Next, the cloth is dyed with natural dyes. Then it is tie-dyed to achieve the intricate designs, normally in orange, yellow, red, brown, black, and purple. Within the region, different ethnic groups produce distinctly different cloths that vary in tightness of weave, color, and embellishments.

BORO-INSPIRED POUF

TIME: All the time in the world

ESTIMATED COST: $40

DIFFICULTY: ✱ ✱

Just like traditional boro textiles, the patchwork sofa in Adam's loft has been made over the course of years spent sewing on patches by hand, layer by layer and stitch by stitch. I love the look and feel of Adam's sofa and really wanted to try my hand at this boro-style upholstery. What's so compelling to me about it, besides how amazing it looks, is that it's always changing—just like new bohemian homes. The boro textile is never complete . . . Also, because the main skill involved here is hand-sewing, you don't have to be versed in the rather complex trade of upholstery to re-cover a chair, sofa, or little pouf. Sweet!

MATERIALS

Cotton pieces. I use old jeans, old work pants, cotton rags, and some fabric scraps left from old projects. All of the fabric I use I find around my home.

A base for the pouf. For the base of this pouf, much like what Adam did with his sofa, I used an old pouf that I bought at Target for $40.

SUPPLIES

Scissors

Needle

Thread. I chose to use white thread because I wanted the hand-stitching to be visible.

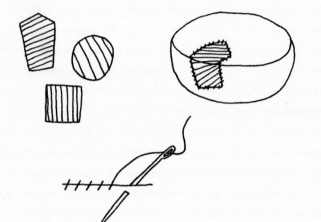

INSTRUCTIONS

1. Cut patches from the cotton pieces. Some should be larger, some smaller. If you like the look of Adam's sofa, with round and square pieces, cut some out rounded and some square. The pieces shouldn't be uniform.

2. One by one, hand-stitch the patches onto the pouf using a whipstitch around the perimeter of the patches. Continue patching and layering until the whole pouf is covered, and then keep on patching if you like! This project has no set finish, so patch to your heart's content!

BORO

Boro is a Japanese folk textile dating from the late 1700s to early 1900s. Literally translated as "rags" or "scraps of cloth," boro textiles are made slowly, from old indigo-dyed cotton rags. Boro futon covers and kimonos are patched and stitched, piece by piece, layer by layer, and handed down from generation to generation; the younger generations continue to add stitches and patches to the "living" textile. While once considered a practical, utilitarian fabric, it is now esteemed as art and is quite collectible. One vendor at the Rose Bowl flea market in Pasadena, California, always has mountains of boro textiles at his stand; I am always temped to come home with a pretty patchworked piece—instead, I now have one that I've made, over many hours, that perhaps my daughter will continue to add patches to as time goes on.

PLANT-O-PEDIA

A HOME AIN'T A HOME WITHOUT PLANTS

I was at my local plant nursery checking out a fern the other day when a beautiful old woman who was eyeing a pothos looked at me and said, "A home ain't a home without plants." I smiled and agreed. I'm still trying to figure out if the nursery planted her there to say that to everyone, or if I was the lone receptor to that sweet sentiment. Regardless, I couldn't agree more. Plants bring to a home what no designer dining table, perfect parquet, or luxe lighting can. Plants breathe life into a room, and they add deep color, bright freshness, and a bold vitality to a space that only something living can bring.

But alas, unlike a designer dining table, plants need sunlight and water, and they can be fussy—fear of being a plant killer deters many people from keeping plants in the home. And that's precisely why I enlisted the help of landscape designer and plant expert Stephanie Bartron to assist in this "plantastic" chapter.

My favorite plants and plant installations from the book are all explained here. So if you fell in love, like I did, with the purple shamrock in Emily and Adam's Portland home (see page 17) or want to replicate the crazemazing terrarium from Arielle's beachfront living room (see page 231), this mini plant-o-pedia will give you all the tools you need to bring these plants into your own home and care for them. It's not about green thumbs or brown thumbs—it's about knowing what the plant needs and fulfilling those needs. So let's get growing!

ARIELLE'S CRAZEMAZING TERRARIUM

MILEECE'S TABLETOP TERRARIUM

GET THE GREEN These terrarium plants are well-matched, needing similar light, water, and temperatures. BLUE FESCUE (*Festuca glauca*). *Graptopetalum kimnachii*. REFLEXED STONECROP (*Sedum reflexum*). **WATER** Water weekly, but let dry between waterings. **SUNLIGHT** Bright direct or indirect light. **PLACEMENT** Small terrariums like this are great on coffee tables, side tables, bookshelves, and desks. **EXTRA CREDIT** Don't overwater! This glass terrarium doesn't have drainage and will hold humidity.

KATHERIN'S AERARIUM

GET THE GREEN AIR PLANT (*Tillandsia*) **WATER** Mist well with a spray bottle two or three times a week, or more often if especially dry, or completely submerge plant in water for a few hours every few weeks. **SUNLIGHT** Bright, filtered light. **PLACEMENT** Since they don't need soil, air plants can be hung from string or wire, placed in a bowl or shell, mounted on a wall, or kept in a terrarium. **EXTRA CREDIT** Air plants can take great temperature fluctuations, but don't let them freeze. Don't water with distilled or softened water—use filtered water or tap water (let it sit first to dissolve chlorine). Water in the morning, not at night, as these "breathe" in carbon (and out oxygen) at night and need to be dry to do so. These plants flower just once, then produce "pups" or plantlets and then die. Gently separate and discard the dead plants.

GET THE GREEN A diverse collection of CACTI, SUCCULENTS, and *Sansevieria* (SNAKE PLANT) **WATER** Water this collection weekly from late spring until late fall, making sure to saturate each little pot. During winter months, water each cactus deeply just once a month. Some, especially the succulents, may prefer a bit more, so give them an extra hit if they look droopy or sad. **SUNLIGHT** Direct sun at some point in the day, in a bright, sunny room. If your curtains are closed until noon, it should be a room that gets afternoon sunlight. **PLACEMENT** These plants photosynthesize in a special way that allows them to absorb CO_2 and release O_2 during the night, so if you have a sunny bedroom, this would be ideal!

They're also dramatic in an entryway or sunny hallway, and you can move the whole collection outside during hot summer months. **EXTRA CREDIT** Remove spent leaves and flowers from succulents to keep them looking fresh. Plan on repotting them as pots fill up, possibly yearly for the succulents—you can also break off stems that are too tall and replant the tops. New roots will form, and they won't look so leggy. Use a very long-necked watering can so that each plant can be watered individually, without you risking getting poked by the many sharp spines. Tape is the best way to remove spines from fingers should you get pricked—gently apply tape to your skin, press down on the affected area, and slowly pull the spines out.

JUSTINA'S CUBBY GARDEN

GET THE GREEN (1) ZANZIBAR GEM or ZZ (*Zamioculcas zamiifolia*) **WATER** Water once a month in the winter, twice a month in the summer. Don't let sit in water. **SUNLIGHT** Shade to partial sun. **PLACEMENT** Does well in low light, so this is a great low-maintenance plant that will do well almost anywhere, even in relatively dark areas of the home. **GET THE GREEN (2)** ICE-BLUE SENECIO (*Senecio serpens*) **WATER** Water regularly but let dry completely between waterings. Water less often in winter. **SUNLIGHT** Bright or indirect sunlight. **PLACEMENT** Hang in a window or place on a windowsill. **GET THE GREEN (3)** STRING OF BANANAS, FISHHOOK SENECIO, BANANA VINE, NECKLACE PLANT (so many names!) (*Senecio radicans*) **WATER** Water weekly or less. Allow to dry out between waterings. **SUNLIGHT** Partial shade outdoors, medium indirect to bright direct light indoors. **PLACEMENT** This is a great easy-care hanging plant for tall shelves, hanging planters, or window boxes. **EXTRA CREDIT** All parts of this plant are poisonous, so keep it out of reach of children and pets. Bring it indoors if temperatures drop below 45°F (7°C).

MILEECE'S TROPICAL WASHROOM

GET THE GREEN (1) AIR PLANT (*Tillandsia*) **GET THE GREEN (2)** BROMELIAD (*Guzmania* variety) **WATER** Keep water in the flower cup, if possible. Water weekly at the base. **SUNLIGHT** Bright, indirect light is best. **PLACEMENT** Great for tabletops and desks. **EXTRA CREDIT** Use bottled or filtered water. The flower can last for several months but will eventually fade. It should be cut off at that point; new plantlets will grow at the base after flowering and the central plant will begin to die. Gently divide new plantlets and discard the spent central plant or replace with a new, flowering plant. **GET THE GREEN (3)** SCHEFFLERA, UMBRELLA TREE (*Brassaia actinophylla*) **WATER** Likes humidity. Water regularly, letting soil dry slightly between waterings. **SUNLIGHT** Bright but indirect light is best. **PLACEMENT** This plant is easy to grow and will get quite large, so give it some room and keep it on the floor. Great for filling a corner in a large room. **EXTRA CREDIT** Umbrella trees are easy to grow, long-lived, and great at cleaning indoor air, but they don't like cold (below 55°F/13°C), so keep them away from windows or drafts, and keep them warm during winter vacations by wrapping them in horticultural fleece, which is available at most home improvement stores.

MATTIE'S STAGHORN FERN

GET THE GREEN STAGHORN FERN (*Platycerium bifurcatum*) **WATER** Water regularly, but infrequently—let it dry out between waterings. Water it by submerging the whole root ball in a bucket or bathtub for 15 minutes weekly and letting it dripdry before rehanging. Mist leaves regularly between waterings unless it is warm and humid. **SUNLIGHT** Bright to medium indirect light. **PLACEMENT** Usually mounted on a piece of wood or cork and hung on the wall, or set in the crook of a tree. These can also be kept in clay pots, where their spores may start growing on the outside of the pot. **EXTRA CREDIT** STAGHORNS prefer humidity and temperatures 60°F–75°F (15°C–24°C), so take it outside only when the temperature is right and the humidity is high. With proper care, they can be very long-lived. Note that they get heavy when wet, so mount well with strong hardware.

SACHA'S SPILLERS

GET THE GREEN (1) SWISS CHEESE PLANT (*Monstera adansonii*) **WATER** Likes water—keep soil moist during spring and summer, then water frequently in fall and winter, but let it dry out a bit between waterings. **SUNLIGHT** Indirect light only. **PLACEMENT** Trailing vines like this should be placed high, but not so high that you can't reach it to water it! Hanging planters and bookshelves are ideal. **EXTRA CREDIT** These can be a little tricky. They prefer warm, humid conditions and don't like temperatures below 60°F (15°C), so keep them away from drafty windows, doors, and air vents. Also feed regularly with plant food from your local garden center. **GET THE GREEN (2)** JADE POTHOS (*Epipremnum aureum*) **WATER** Water weekly, letting soil dry to the touch between waterings. **SUN-LIGHT** Prefers shade, so bright indirect light or a dark room. **PLACEMENT** This easy-care plant is perfect for offices and darker corners. Place high so it can drape down; vining stems reach 12"–24" (30–60 cm) or more. **EXTRA CREDIT** This is one of the many houseplants that are toxic, if ingested, to both cats and dogs, so keep it out of reach if your pets are plant munchers. Otherwise, this is a very easy plant to grow—you can root cuttings in a glass of water to make more, and it's good at cleaning your indoor air. Pinch back and/or thin stems as needed to keep it lush and full.

ALEA'S STRING OF HEARTS

GET THE GREEN ROSARY VINE, STRING OF HEARTS (*Ceropegia woodii*) **WATER** Somewhat succulent, so use care never to overwater or allow the plant to sit in water. Water thoroughly, but allow the soil to completely dry out before watering again. **SUN-LIGHT** Full sun is OK, if some protection is provided during the hottest part of the day. Prefer summer temperatures 70°F–75°F (21°C–24°C), but during the winter, when the plant goes dormant, it should be kept in a cooler room, if possible—60°F–65°F (15°C–18°C). **PLACEMENT** Each vine will reach 2'–4' (0.6–1.2 m) in length; the plant should be hung or set on a pedestal where it will receive bright light for most of the day. **EXTRA CREDIT** You'll find that hummingbirds are attracted to the flowers, if your plant is hung in your garden during the summer months.

PAIGE'S & EMILY'S JADE PLANTS

GET THE GREEN JADE PLANT (*Crassula ovata*) **WATER** Allow to dry between waterings, keeping the soil moderately dry. During the winter months, water less, but do not let it overdry. **SUNLIGHT** Direct sunlight for part of the day. **PLACEMENT** Southern window where it will receive at least four hours of direct sunlight. **EXTRA CREDIT** Move away from windows at night during the winter to avoid injury from the cold.

ALEA'S WINDOW GARDEN

GET THE GREEN (1) COLUMN CACTUS, PERU-VIAN TORCH (*Cereus peruvianus*) **WATER** Weekly or less—soil should dry between waterings and plant should become slightly spongy, then plump again after watering. **SUNLIGHT** Bright direct or indirect light, indoors. Outdoors, keep in full sun to partial shade (while temperatures are above 50°F/10°C). **PLACEMENT** Plant in a heavy, stable pot, as this cactus is top-heavy and will break if knocked over. Best on the floor, perhaps between a window and a chair or couch. **EXTRA CREDIT** Older cacti produce stunning, fragrant flowers that open at night. **GET THE GREEN (2)** ELEPHANT EAR, TARO (*Colocasia* varieties) **WATER** These love water! Water regularly and keep soil moist (but not soggy). Great for humid areas and rooms such as large, sunny bathrooms. If air is dry, spray water on leaves often, run a cool-mist humidifier nearby, and/or place the plant on a pebble-and-water-filled saucer so roots don't sit in water but the humidity around the plant is increased. **SUNLIGHT** Bright, indirect light. **PLACEMENT** This plant can get big—between 3' and 5' (0.9–1.5 m) tall and wide, so give it space. It makes a good room divider or large focal point and is best on the floor or on a sturdy side table, as the tuber and plant can get heavy. **EXTRA CREDIT** Leaves may die if temperatures fall below 60°F (15°C). If

this happens, set aside in cool, dark place until springtime, letting soil dry out, but take care that the plant does not freeze. As temperatures rise, new leaves should sprout from the rhizome. Note that these are poisonous to cats and dogs, and to humans, if eaten raw. Sap can also irritate the skin.

ADAM & PAIGE'S FIDDLE-LEAF FIGS

GET THE GREEN FIDDLE-LEAF FIG (*Ficus lyrata*) **WATER** Water when just the top 1" (2.5 cm) or so of soil is dry. **SUNLIGHT** Bright, indirect light. **PLACEMENT** These trees are native to warm, humid, tropical places with consistent moisture and even temperatures. The more you can mimic their natural environment, the happier they'll be. **EXTRA CREDIT** These trees will lean toward the light, so rotate them every few weeks to keep a uniform shape.

MILEECE'S WHITE BIRD

GET THE GREEN WHITE BIRD-OF-PARADISE (*Strelitzia nicolai*) **WATER** Water regularly, but let soil surface dry between waterings. **SUNLIGHT** Bright direct or indirect light. **PLACEMENT** On the floor in a big pot. Good as a room divider or to fill a sunny corner. **EXTRA CREDIT** Cut off spent leaves at base of plant. Keep warm in winter; this plant dislikes temperatures below 60°F (15°C). Older plants may have dramatic white flowers and will grow new plants from the base. Divide, as needed, to keep the plant from overcrowding.

ADAM'S & KERBY'S SPLIT-LEAF PHILODENDRONS

GET THE GREEN SPLIT-LEAF PHILODEN-DRON, FRUIT SALAD PLANT (*Monstera deliciosa*) **WATER** Water regularly, but let the top 1" (2.5 cm) of soil dry completely between waterings. Water less in winter. **SUNLIGHT** Moderate to bright indirect light. **PLACEMENT** Unlike the trailing SWISS CHEESE PLANT (*Monstera adansonii*) (above left), which is of the same genus, this is a big, upright plant that looks great on the floor in a big statement pot, either next to a wall or as a room divider. **EXTRA CREDIT** Aerial roots will grow from the stem—tuck those that will reach into the soil and secure upper roots to a planting stake. Wipe leaves regularly with a soft cloth to reduce dust and keep them glossy. Note that all parts of this plant are poisonous to both people and pets.

EMILY'S RUBBER TREE

GET THE GREEN VARIEGATED RUBBER TREE (*Ficus elastica* 'Variegata') **WATER** Keep moist but not soggy in spring and summer; let soil surface dry between waterings in fall and winter. **SUNLIGHT** Bright to medium indirect light. **PLACEMENT** This gets big, so it's usually best in a big pot on the floor. When young (and small) it works on a speaker or side table, filling a corner nicely. **EXTRA CREDIT** Regularly wipe the leaves with a damp cloth to remove dust and keep them glossy.

MILEECE'S BROMELIAD

GET THE GREEN URN PLANT, BROMELIAD (*Aechmea fasciata* 'Primera') **WATER** Keep water in the flower cup, if possible. Water weekly at the base. **SUNLIGHT** Bright indirect light, or direct morning or evening light. **PLACEMENT** Great for side tables and large shelves. **EXTRA CREDIT** Use bottled or filtered water. The flower can last for several months but will eventually fade; it should be cut off at that point. New plantlets will grow at the base after flowering, and the central plant will begin to die. Gently divide new plantlets and discard spent central plant, or replace with a new, flowering plant.

EMILY'S SHAMROCK

GET THE GREEN SHAMROCK PLANT (*Oxalis hybrid*) **WATER** Frequent light watering—just enough to keep plant moist but not soggy. **SUNLIGHT** Bright to moderate indirect light. **PLACEMENT** Great tabletop or shelf plant for a bright kitchen or office, where half-finished water glasses can be drizzled on them daily.

ALEA'S CORAL

GET THE GREEN JADE PLANT (*Crassula ovata* 'Coral') **WATER** Water regularly, but let soil dry between waterings. Water less in winter. **SUNLIGHT** Bright direct or indirect light. **PLACEMENT** This is a dramatic tabletop specimen. **EXTRA CREDIT** May flower in early spring. Keep above 50°F (10°C) in winter.

Resources

HOMES

Below is a list of the owners whose homes you've just seen, along with their social media contact information.

EMILY KATZ & ADAM PORTERFIELD
@emily_katz
emilykatz.com
@goldenruledesign
goldenruledesign.com

JOSIE MARAN & ALI ALBORZI
@JosieMaranCosmetics
josiemarancosmetics.com

MARIKA WAGLE
@marikawagle

KATHERIN & BRIAN SMIRKE
gypsan.com
baskicg.com
@domeinthedesert

ANNE PARKER & ALEA JOY
@aleajoy
solabeeflowers.com
@anne_parker
madebyanneparker.com

MILEECE PETRE
mileece.is

EMILY BAKER & KERBY FERRIS
@lavendermirror
@swordandfern
swordandfern.com

STELLA & PEDRO ALBERTI
@StellaAlberti
stellaalberticouture.com

FAITH BLAKENEY
@FaithBlakeney
callmefaith.com

MATTIE KANNARD & DENNIS SMITH
@MattieKannard
rattiemae.tumblr.com

PAIGE MORSE
@Paige_Morse
paigemorsecreative.com

MICHELA GOLDSCHMIED
@LadyGold58

AMHALISE MORGAN
@Amhalise
amhalise.com

SACHA PYTKA
@sachapytka

ERICA TANOV
ericatanov.com

JARED FRANK
@jrdfrnk
topsydesign.com

ARIELLE PYTKA
@ariellepytka

LOUISE INGALLS STURGES & TYLER HAMMOND BRODIE
@besosyfotos
@popular_delusions
casualrainbow.com

ADAM POGUE
@mrpoguemahone

JUSTINA BLAKENEY & JASON ROSENCRANTZ
@justinablakeney
blog.justinablakeney.com

RETAIL

Here are some of my favorite sources for inspiration and great stuff, both online and in stores.

ABC CARPET & HOME, NEW YORK, abchome.com

ANTHROPOLOGIE
anthropologie.com

BABASOUK, BABASOUK.CA

BADIA DESIGN, LOS ANGELES
badiadesign.com

BLACKMAN CRUZ, LOS ANGELES
blackmancruz.com

BRICK LANE MARKET, LONDON
visitbricklane.org

BROOKLYN FLEA MARKET, BROOKLYN
brooklynflea.com

BROOME ST. GENERAL, LOS ANGELES
broomestgeneral.com

BUILD IT GREEN!, NEW YORK
bignyc.org

CALYPSO HOME
calypsostbarth.com/home

CANVAS, NEW YORK
canvashomestore.com

CATBIRD, NEW YORK
catbirdnyc.com

CB2, cb2.com

CLAR'S AUCTION GALLERY, OAKLAND, CA, clars.com

COYOTE TRADERS LAS CRUCES, LAS CRUCES
A long-standing store with vintage and rustic furniture and colorful Talavera pottery.

CRAIGSLIST, Craigslist.org

DEKOR, LOS ANGELES
dekorla.com

DEL SOL INTERNATIONAL SHOPS, NEW MEXICO AND ARIZONA, delsolstores.com

EBAY, ebay.com

ECOHOME IMPROVEMENT, BERKELEY, CA
ecohomeimprovement.com

ERICA TANOV, BERKELEY/ NEW YORK, ericatanov.com

ESPIONAGE, LOS ANGELES
espionagela.com

ETSY, etsy.com
Among the thousands of amazing shops on this site, these are some of my favorites: /WOMANSHOPSWORLD, /WEAREMFEO, /ETHANOLLIE, /SUKAN, /BOUTIQUEMAROC

GALERI AZUL, MESILLA, NM
An enchanting collection of folk art with a focus on Day of the Dead, handmade masks, Mexican hammered silver mirrors, and woven tapestries.

HERNANDEZ, LOS ANGELES
A furniture store specializing in vintage mid-century modern pieces.

HIDDEN TREASURES, LOS ANGELES
A huge stock that's always rotating, from glass beads to cashmere sweaters and perfectly flared denim.

IKEA, ikea.com

JF CHEN, LOS ANGELES
jfchen.com

JM DRYGOODS, AUSTIN, TX
jmdrygoods.com

JUST ONE EYE, LOS ANGELES
justoneeye.com

KNEELAND MERCADO
kneelandmercado.com

L'AVIVA HOME, NEW YORK
lavivahome.com

LONG BEACH FLEA MARKET, LONG BEACH, CA
longbeachantiquemarket.com

LOWELL, PORTLAND, OR
lowellportland.com

MAISON MIDI, LOS ANGELES
maison-midi.com

MARCHE AUX PUCES (PARIS FLEA MARKET), PARIS
These legendary markets have everything from antiques to junk, trinkets to collectibles, and new to vintage clothing.

MARIMEKKO
marimekko.com

MAVEN COLLECTIVE, PORTLAND, OR
mavencollectivepdx.com

MESILLA BOOK CENTER, MESILLA, NM
Specializing in books about New Mexico and the Southwest, they also have a wide selection of Southwestern jewelry and pottery.

MICHAEL LEVINE, LOS ANGELES
lowpricefabric.com

NANNIE INEZ, AUSTIN, TX
nannieinez.com

NEW HIGH MART, LOS ANGELES
newhighmart.com

NICKEY KEHOE, LOS ANGELES
nickeykehoe.com

OBSOLETE, VENICE, CA
obsoleteinc.com

OLDE GOOD THINGS, LOS ANGELES/NEW YORK
oldegoodthings.com

ONE KINGS LANE
onekingslane.com

OSBORNE & LITTLE, LOS ANGELES
osborneandlittle.com

PASADENA CITY COLLEGE FLEA MARKET, PASADENA, CA
pasadena.edu/fleamarket/

POWELL'S, PORTLAND, OR
powellsbooks.com

PLATFORM EXPERIMENT, LOS ANGELES
theplatformexperiment.com

PLUMO, plumo.com

PROJECT BLY, projectbly.com

ROLLING GREENS, LOS ANGELES
rollinggreensnursery.com

ROSE BOWL FLEA MARKET, PASADENA/LOS ANGELES
rgcshows.com

SERENA & LILY
serenaandlily.com

SHOPCLASS, LOS ANGELES
shopclassla.com

SOLABEE, PORTLAND, OR
solabeeflowers.com

SPROUT HOME, BROOKLYN/CHICAGO, sprouthome.com

ST. VINCENT DE PAUL THRIFT STORE, LOS ANGELES
svdpla.org

STEVEN ALAN HOME, NEW YORK, stevenalan.com

TAIL OF THE YAK, BERKELEY
Full of fantasy and whimsy, this shop offers new and antique decorative arts, gifts, jewelry, and other treasures.

TERRAIN, shopterrain.com

THE END OF HISTORY, NEW YORK
theendofhistoryshop.blogspot.com

THE LOADED TRUNK
loadedtrunk.com

THE WINDOW, LOS ANGELES
thewindowla.com

THOMAS HAYES, LOS ANGELES
thomashayesgallery.com

THUNDERBIRD DE LA MESILLA, MESILLA, NM
Housed in the oldest brick building in New Mexico, built in 1863, they offer a wide selection of folk art from Mexico, as well as Native American and Southwest jewelry, pottery, kachina dolls, and storytellers.

TOAST UK, toa.st

WEST ELM, westelm.com

WHITE ELEPHANT ANTIQUES, DALLAS, whiteelephantantiqueswarehouse.com

WHITE SANDS TRADING COMPANY, ALAMOGORDO, NM
whitesandstradingcompany.com

Hanging Planter Template

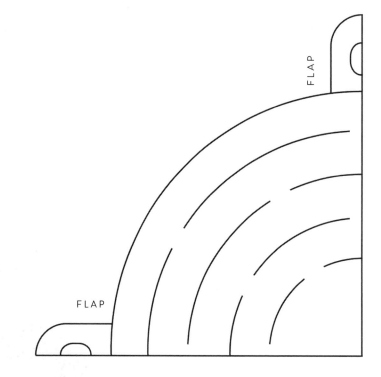

FLAP

FLAP

BODY PIECE A

Suzani Pillow Templates

CIRCLE TEMPLATE A

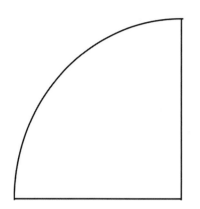

SMALL FLOWERS TEMPLATES

FLOWER TEMPLATES

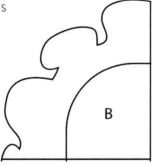

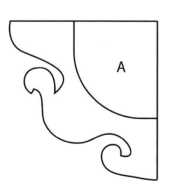

ROUNDED RECTANGULAR RING TEMPLATE

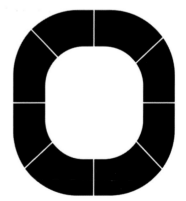

ACKNOWLEDGMENTS

It takes a village to raise a child, and to make a book, too. This labor of love would never have come to fruition if it weren't for a whole slew of extremely talented people I love. I have so much to be grateful for.

First, I have to thank DABITO for working on this with me and for making it so dang pretty. Your talent, eye, and supremely chill vibe made this book. I love you so much. To my hot husband, JASON—thank you for keeping me inspired, for always supporting me in all of my creative projects, and for being the best daddy in the world to our sweet Ida. You were also the first to read, edit, and keep it real with me on the book. I love you, and I couldn't have made this book without you. To NATALIE GLUCK MITCHELL, for project managing the book, talking me back from the ledge on numerous occasions, and for your meticulous crafting skills—I love you! To SARA BAUER for tirelessly and passionately helping to find all of these incredible homes and for assisting on location. To my agent, STEFANIE VON BORSTEL, for believing in my far-out ideas and to DERVLA KELLY, thank you for believing in me and in this project.

To STEPHANIE BARTRON for lending me your plantastic knowledge and time. To KATIE WILSON, thank you for the lightning fast (and totally adorable) DIY illustrations. To MONICA RAMOS, for the illustrations in the front and back endpapers of the book—you inspire!

To SHANNON and FAITH for always being an ear to bounce ideas off of. To my MOM and DAD, to my GRANDPARENTS, to MARY and JIM and DENNY and BRENDA, thank you for taking such amazing care of Ida, for **always** being there for Jason and me, for the enthusiasm, and for the unconditional love.

To my UNCLE MIKE and TANTE JAN, thank you for generously handing over your beautiful home to shoot our DIY projects. Thank you to CAITLIN, KEARNEN, and CASEY for letting us stay at your homes while shooting.

To my editor, ANDREA DANESE—in you I have found a mentor and a friend, thank you for generously lending your expertise, vision, and general good vibes to me and to the project. To the whole crew at ABRAMS, especially to the incredible book designer, DEB WOOD, thank you for letting this book be an accurate representation of my vision, only making it look even better (and cleaner!) than I could have ever imagined.

A heartfelt thanks to YOU new bohemians, who let us into your homes, cooked us meals, gave us sweet little what-nots, and shared your lives, creativity, and families with us. You are this book.

And to you, MY FAITHFUL READERS, who are always a voice of support and encouragement. This book would not be in your hands if it weren't for you.

Lastly, thank you to my little IDA for letting Mama travel around the world to make this book and for making me ever more excited to come home to you.